Information Technology and World Politics

Information Technology and World Politics

Edited by Michael J. Mazarr

First published 2002 by
PALGRAVE MACMILLAN™
175 Fifth Avenue, New York, N.Y. 10010 and
Houndmills, Basingstoke, Hampshire, England RG21 6XS.
Companies and representatives throughout the world.

PALGRAVE MACMILLAN is the global academic imprint of the Palgrave
Macmillan division of St. Martin's Press, LLC and of Palgrave Macmillan Ltd.
Macmillan® is a registered trademark in the United States, United Kingdom and
other countries. Palgrave is a registered trademark in the European Union and other
countries.

ISBN 1–4039–6057–7 hardback

Library of Congress Cataloging-in-Publication Data

Information technology and world politics / Michael J. Mazarr, editor.
    p. cm.
  Includes bibliographical references and index.
  ISBN 1–4039–6057–7
    1. Information technology—Economic aspects. 2. Information technology—
Political aspects. I. Mazarr, Michael J., 1965-

HC79.I55 I5393 2002
303.48'33—dc21

2002068421

A catalogue record for this book is available from the British Library.

Design by Autobookcomp.

First edition: November 2002
10 9 8 7 6 5 4 3 2 1

Printed in the United States of America.

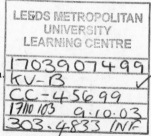

Contents

CHAPTER 1

Introduction:
Information Technology and World
Politics—The Growing Connection

Michael J. Mazarr

This volume examines a subject that has so far received scant attention, at least in terms of formal, rigorous research projects: the effect of information technology on world politics, and specifically the growing role of the Internet in promoting freedom and changing social and political norms. There is no question that the connection is increasingly important and potentially profound, but beyond those crude initial truisms, not much is known for certain about the subject. Much of the writing on it remains dominated by classic first-phase analysis, drawing sweeping conclusions and making bold predictions on the basis of more hunch than evidence. This volume is an attempt to take a further step in the direction of understanding.

There are some obvious reasons to find import in the intersection of the technology to disseminate information and the character of the international system. The Internet has already begun to revolutionize the conduct of business and government; its effect on world politics may end up being equally as significant. History provides ample evidence, from the origins of the printing press to the role of the television in Eastern Europe in the late 1980s, for the proposition that the sudden widening of information access can have ripple effects throughout societies. A handful of suggestive case studies, several of them described in this book, provide tantalizing hints of the potential role of such technologies as the Internet and cell phones in promoting political reform and change in closed societies.

But there is an even deeper and more underlying connection at work here—the tie between information technology and world politics on the one hand and the process of globalization on the other.

The Internet would have had a substantial effect on world politics under any circumstance. In the context of globalization, that effect is magnified many times. A globalizing world is already one racing through rapid change, already feeling the effects of the spread of information and relationships, already confronting questions of cultural identity and political control. The Internet and other emerging information technologies accelerate this process, deepen it, exacerbate its destabilizing effects, and sometimes become the scapegoats for those effects.

The global spread of information, communications, and high-technology development—and the social, economic, and cultural changes that come with it—are generating both local instabilities and globe-spanning tensions. From burgeoning anti-Americanism among Chinese young people who fear cultural assault (and yet who express their views in Internet chat rooms) to stresses within U.S. alliances to potent mixtures of cultural and economic instability in the Middle East, technoglobalization with an American tinge may be the most important single author of U.S. security challenges in the next decade. The events of September 11 would certainly seem to suggest that this is the case.

As Samuel Huntington and other theorists of the phenomenon recognized decades ago, modernization is a destabilizing force—inexorable, homogenizing, opposed to tradition, uprooting cultures whole-sale in favor of the new, modern way of organizing society. Globalization has now tended to both magnify and institutionalize the traditional effects of modernization. International financial agencies demand rapid and complete adherence to free-market economic policies. Global aid organizations invest in and speed up the extension of literacy to whole populations. Leading democracies push for rapid political and economic liberalization in still-closed societies. All of this tends to make an already wrenching process even more so.

It is under the shadow of these larger trends that the Internet has begun intersecting with world politics in exciting, turbulent, and potentially destabilizing ways. This is true especially in its effect on the process of democratization underway throughout the post-Soviet regions and the developing world, including such major world powers as China and India, and its growing connection to nationalist movements across the globe.

Information technologies have already helped to advance democracy in key countries around the world. From Indonesia to Malaysia to Mexico to China, the Internet has spread information, allowed nongovernmental groups to coordinate activities, and prompted grassroots activism in opposition to centralized authority. Partly as a result, debates on the freedom of the Internet are already underway—among governments, nongovernmental organizations (NGOs), corporations, other groups, and individual citizens—in these and other countries.

The link between democratization and open flows of information is hardly new. This basic link was the justification, after all, for such cold war information initiatives as Radio Free Europe. But the Internet has given an old connection new bite, and the implications and trends associated with this shift need to be better understood.

So, too, do the emerging effects of the Internet and other information technologies on the far side of the democratization process, past the initial overturning of dictatorship and into the hard work of fashioning a new democratic system. The process of building a democracy is fraught with transitional risks, and in fact countries in the transition to democracy make war more often than authoritarian states or established democracies. The process of democratization can go right, creating a robust civil society, the rule of law, and true freedom; or it can go wrong in a dozen ways, from xenophobic nationalism to military-dominated praetorianism to a complete return to autocratic rule. Such perilous transitions have been under way for over a decade in the areas of the former Soviet Bloc. They have begun, in a different form, throughout the quasi-closed societies of Asia, including China. The first hints of a similar process can be seen in the Arab world.

Information technologies, led by the Internet, are sure to have a profound effect on these processes of reform and change. They could provide the means for nationalist groups to spread their exclusionary message and recruit followers. They could give citizens of a country or region access to global news and opinion, and thereby undermine the arguments of local despots or demagogues. The emerging technologies of the information revolution are likely to shape the global trend toward democratization in important ways over the coming decade.

What is less clear is just what this effect will be. Some observers believe (and hope) that the Internet will prove to be the most effective information-spreading medium of all and that widespread access to it will advance freedom even more rapidly than earlier telecommunications and information technologies such as radio and television. Others worry that people browsing the Net for information have no way of judging the objectivity or accuracy of what they find. And there is no question that extremist, violent groups already use the Internet to promote their cause, in ways ranging from disseminating their message to raising funds to trading messages and planning attacks.

The spread of the Internet will also have economic implications, and these could play important roles in encouraging or undermining development, liberalization, and democratization in key countries. Advocates see the Internet as a gateway into the global economy for developing countries, a way to nurture local, cutting-edge industries without needing years of foreign investment and the presence of multinational corporations in advance. With the right education and language skills, people anywhere can theoretically find "virtual" or "free agent" work online; companies could put together project teams from many countries. The Internet could, then, be a way to find and utilize underdeveloped talent in developing nations.

That hopeful vision requires that there be talent to find, however, and it also demands widespread Internet connectivity—and therefore a sophisticated telecommunications infrastructure—in the target nations. Effective and widespread education, and in many cases rigorous foreign language training, remain preconditions for Internet-enabled development, and many developing nations remain far from this goal. As several of the chapters that follow will document, moreover, Internet penetration rates outside the most advanced economies remain depressingly low. In some cases, undemocratic governments have placed further barriers in the way of broad Internet access for their populations. And one author even discusses a possible downside of Internet-encouraged economic activity: Skilled labor in developing nations might use the Net as a way to find jobs in the United States or other developed areas, generating a Net-sparked brain drain of the very people who possess the talents and Net access that would make possible local progress empowered by the new technology.

One of the primary values of the chapters that follow is the range of perspectives they offer on these and related questions. In response to the first, often simplistic assertions about the role of information technology (especially the Internet) in such processes as democratization and development, the authors raise a number of complex and sometimes paradoxical issues. If the analysis and case studies that follow are any indication, the Internet is likely to carry many contradictory implications.

In the area of freedom and democracy, the Internet may indeed help promote freedom, but only in the right circumstances and perhaps in narrower and more limited ways than was first hoped. Authoritarian regimes may indeed be able to slow the democratizing effect of the new medium—but not forever, and never completely. Some repressive governments (and even, increasingly, free ones as well) may be able to employ the Internet as a tool to monitor their citizens, even as global NGOs use it to keep better track of the actions of those same governments. Arguments about the optimal form of democracy will rage on the Net, which may end up strengthening the universalistic, Western-style side of the debate—or else the particularistic Asian, African, and Latin American response to Westernization. It is simply too soon to tell.

In terms of ethnicity and identity, some people going online in search of an ethnic or tribal or religious identity may find it; others may be deflected from the pursuit of group identity into an embrace of a broader perspective. Some might discover that a virtual identification allows them to live more comfortably in a plural, tolerant, globalized country while still maintaining a traditional tie; others may be inspired by their virtual group identity to challenge or break away from the state within whose political boundaries they reside. Diasporas may be empowered or undermined by access to Internet-based chat rooms, information reservoirs, and calls to action. Governments or nongovernmental groups attempting to rally global support to an ethnic, religious, or cultural cause on the Net may find success, or they may see their message swamped with thousands of web-based counterarguments and contrary facts.

There are dozens of possible results, and combinations of results, of the Internet's intersection with a globalizing world. We are only beginning to understand the complicated potential of this new medium. An especially interesting issue involves the intersection of evolving youth attitudes in key developing countries and an Internet-prompted free flow of sometimes nationalistic information. There is some evidence of a growth in nationalistic sentiment among young people in such countries as Malaysia, Thailand, Germany, China, and Russia. As these young men and women increasingly rely on the Internet for information and communications, they will gain access to varying cultures and points of view—and, at the same time, a growing number of web sites promoting xenophobic, exclusive nationalism. Which way the Net eventually shepherds them, if it has such a clear-cut effect at all, may be critical in shaping their view, the flavor of politics in their countries, and by extension the future of world politics.

Substantial research has been done since about the mid-1990s on various aspects of these questions, but the first definitive analytical marker on these questions has yet to be laid down. Much of the early research has been suggestive and anecdotal—a long-time China-watcher putting her oar into the Internet issue, for example, or a journalist doing a series of short pieces on recent news events. Many existing country studies on democratization are in the conflict resolution and rule of law traditions; few if any focus on the role of information technology.

This book has a simple purpose: to provide detailed snapshots of a few specific case studies and issues in the hope of advancing the dialogue about the growing connection between the Internet and world politics. Perhaps the most common underlying theme is to beware of easy assumptions. The Internet and related information technologies are neither as benign nor as potentially destructive as some breathless early pronouncements suggested.

Glenn McCormick, Emil Bailey, and Tania O'Neil discuss the broad intersection between nationalism, identity, and the Internet and conclude that its effect is likely to be complicated and varied. All display some degree of skepticism of the notion that the Internet will create an information-based "global village" of shared values and habits. Glenn Hickok worries about the national security vulnerabilities created by the use of Internet-related technologies for a specific purpose—the reliance on satellite-based Internet access. His chapter provides yet more warnings that seemingly obvious benefits could turn out to have hidden complications and dangers.

In a series of case studies, Richard Hughes, Alessandra Cabras, Robert Peters, and Michael Rabasco point to the undeniable potential of the Internet (and other technologies; Cabras focuses on cell phones) to promote the flow of information and the spread of democracy in closed societies. Broadly, several of the chapters do point to the ways in which Internet-based communications and information have encouraged individuals and groups pushing for greater freedom. But they also make clear that the story is far from a simple or linear one; that in some cases, repressive governments can use the Internet for their own purposes; and that in others, clever regimes are finding ways to restrict the allowed dialogue, even on the Net.

Finally, three authors—Sudhir Mahara, Ryan McMichael, and Amanda Olson—discuss the connection between the Internet and economic development. Again, they endorse some degree of hopefulness that, in some circumstances, Internet-based economic ties could supplement more traditional avenues to development. But again, their combined message is a mixed one—a story of clear opportunities, but ones limited by the existing economic and infrastructure base of the countries and other factors.

Each of these authors is approaching a fresh topic. A number of them, for example, had to rely on interviews and e-mail exchanges to gather some suggestive data on issues where no large-scale research has yet been done. All of them are working on questions that inevitably invite more speculation than empirical proof. They would surely all agree with one notion—that the Internet's ultimate impact on world politics will only be known for certain in retrospect. There are too many uncertainties, too many complex interactions underway, to make any simple forecasts.

Will the Internet accelerate political reform in China? Will it jump-start development in Africa? Will it bind together ethnic diasporas around the world—and if it does so, will those groups thereby become more or less satisfied with the political entities where they reside? Will it become a reservoir of human commonality or difference?

These are big questions—some of the most important that international relations theorists and practitioners will confront in coming years as they think about the evolving character of world politics. No one knows the answers. This situation calls for a sustained, rigorous focus on these and related issues; with this book, the authors hope to make a contribution to that end.

PART ONE

Information Technology and the "Global Village"

CHAPTER 2

Stateless Nations:
"I Pledge Allegiance To . . . ?"

Glenn McCormick

Man is a social being, even if not always sociable. The desire to commune and interact with some group defined as "us" and exclude "them" has been a driving force throughout history. The end game, so far, has been the consolidation of this social-ism (as a trait, not party) as politics into the state, meaning the construction and acceptance of a joint form of central government over a given physical domain. This condition of statehood is in flux throughout the world. At different times and places, nations—as defined by ethnicity or language or race—have found themselves stateless. That is to say, they have no plot of land with recognized and defined borders where they live under their own rules and government free from dominion or suzerainty.

These stateless nations have reacted to their situation along the spectrum of possible responses, but violence, at some point, has often been one consequence. Whether one examines Armenians under the Turks, the Basque in Spain, the Kurds of Iran, Iraq, and Turkey, the Irish under the British, the Romani in Eastern Europe, the Jewish Diaspora, or the Palestinians under Israel—the evidence of the desire to maintain a sense of nationhood strongly manifests itself over generations.

In this era of globalization, the effect of the Internet can be to both accentuate and ease this national cleavage, this sense of us and other. When even established states fear the loss of their identities to the homogenizing effects of massive flows of trade and people, the loss to humanity of the richness of the human experience as embodied in and by the variety of national identities—languages and cultures—would be incalculable. My purpose here is to examine some of the effects the Internet has on both how nations maintain solidarity in spite of lacking the advantages of statehood (in the face of some states' active discouragement) and how it may mitigate or exacerbate the desire or necessity for the plot of land they can claim as home.

If the Internet can provide a canvas upon which nations can paint their social, linguistic, cultural, and political beliefs, then perhaps the physical struggle for safe cultural havens and borders may no longer be as necessary for their preservation or evolution. Yet the same inherent capability of the Internet may have the opposite effect: Where nations have cultural havens within countries, the active use of the Net by these stateless groups attempting to create or solidify political identities, in a perceived need to maintain their uniqueness, could diminish the trend toward global integration. The degree with which these nations have availed themselves of alternative methods, facilitated through the Net, to preserve linguistic and cultural traits, maintain contacts with wide-flung elements of their respective diasporas, and exhibit elements of self-governance may indicate the degree to which their survival remains affixed to a physical homeland and political structure.

Cultural Nations

The past decade has seen the creation of a number of individual and joint governmental-like structures around the world, designed for an equally impressive number of purposes.[1] The massive proliferation of nongovernmental organizations (NGOs) reflects the need and desire for people to achieve an end or ends in lieu of, or in spite of, traditional governmental entities. Some NGOs should more properly be called extragovernmental organizations, as they can satisfy needs traditionally under the purview of governments. The manner in which indigenous peoples and other stateless nations have facilitated the Internet mirrors that of NGOs in their various calls for action and the dissemination of information. To the extent that a nation is defined by its culture, the need to preserve its language, heritage, and cohesiveness should be reflected on the Internet: The organizing schema, as it evolves and matures on the Net, can become a virtual political or governing—in the sense of directing—entity that can draw on the target peoples' loyalties.

The native tribes and other indigenous peoples of the Americas have been active in such efforts. Mostly decimated by the actions of the colonizing invaders, today they have neither the numbers nor the distinct regional homelands on the basis of which a dramatic reassertion of sovereign political rights could be claimed. Before many of these native languages and cultures disappear forever, several organizations have sprouted in the attempt to both save them and help them flourish—and increasingly, they are using the Internet to achieve their goals.

The Indigenous Language Institute, created in 1992, has the expressed purpose of revitalizing the use of American native languages. Directed by Native Americans, the institute is primarily a clearinghouse of information—but does sponsor seminars and surveys to determine the state of affairs.

> The Indigenous Language Institute (ILI) recognizes the imminent loss of indigenous peoples' languages and acknowledges the individuality of indigenous communities. ILI facilitates innovative, successful community-based initiatives for language revitalization through collaboration with other appropriate groups and organizations, and promotes public awareness of this crisis.[2]

A creature of the Internet, ILI uses its presence on the Net to facilitate the maintenance and salvation of dying languages. Success stories are published, intended to inspire the troops to reverse the tide of loss. The ILI's Native Language Revitalization Resource Database lists 63 different tribal dialects, from Apache to Zuni, with active language schools—a surprising number of which are less than 15 years old.[3] Though not created by the Net, the ease with which information and interest is disseminated and accessed through the Net could arguably have aided the creation of such schools.

Another Internet site, both academic and practical in nature, also seeks to preserve and enhance the spread of threatened languages. SIL International had its beginnings over 50 years ago; it trains individuals to become teachers of these endangered languages in an attempt to spread their usage and viability. Primarily concerned with the preservation of nonwritten languages, SIL has nonetheless been instrumental in the transliteration of languages to aid in the goal of teaching and preservation. SIL created a web presence in 1998 and has found the web a valuable tool to assist in its efforts at both education and discovery. Academic treatises sponsored by the institute recognize the impact of the Internet and attempt to identify possible pitfalls and suggest methods by which threatened languages can become living—or at least not as moribund—through the web. One example of the problems discussed is the tagging of web addresses so that the page is accessed in the proper language.[4]

The institute is also interested in the written word on the web. To this end, the institute is a focal point in the creation and dissemination of applicable fonts. They provide 123 different fonts for both Windows and Mac applications, covering languages from Albanian to Yi, including rarely used fonts designed for Navajo, Tatar, and Cree.

> The information technology (IT) industry has been driven in recent years to address problems of multilingualism and internationalization. This has been driven to a significant extent by the growth of the Internet. Rapidly increasing economic development throughout the world, together with the growth of the 'Net, has actually resulted in a significant increase in the number of languages that technologies need to support. In many parts of the world, speakers of previously "unknown" languages (that is, unknown to speakers of "major" languages) are beginning to make their mark on the World Wide Web and are using their own languages to do so.[5]

There are numerous other efforts with the stated purpose of language preservation that have a web presence.[6] A related question is whether or not the special identification a group's language and other cultural attributes give them translates into an enhanced political identity.

Virtual Political Nations

> The First Nations Peoples of this land governed their affairs for centuries. Their unique customs, languages, and way of life were intrinsically tied to the lands they occupied. It is not a story, not a fictitious tall tale, but historical fact. The Assembly of First Nations (AFN) strives to present and preserve the authenticity of North American history with the goal of enhancing justice for the aboriginal peoples of Canada. Fighting for long standing First Nations rights is not merely a fight for natural resources and self-determination; it is also a fight for human rights, human dignity, and cultural survival. It is a struggle for

those truths, which are so outstanding and self-evident that they render any challenge to them as being absurd and beyond all enlightened reason.[7]

The previous passage is a manifestation of the growing political awareness and clout of one type of stateless nation. The indigenous tribes of the Americas have found new voice for both their immediate and long-slumbering concerns through collective efforts. AFN is a Canadian organization but has set itself up as a virtual government-in-exile to defend the rights of and seek redress for all the native peoples of North America. The explicit justifications for their efforts derive from the belief that "the Creator gave us our spiritual belief, our languages, our cultures . . . " and that "we have maintained our freedom, our languages, and our traditions from time immemorial."[8] In other words, by depending upon cultural and linguistic identity to define themselves rather than a specific plot of land, the first nations seek to reestablish a degree of political control over themselves. It is of interest to note that until their collective disenfranchisement, many of these nations were my no means aligned with each other and were otherwise unrelated.

Acknowledging further the strength in numbers maxim, the Assembly of First Nations has joined forces with the National Council of American Indians (NCAI) and other indigenous groups from all the Americas. Just in March 2001, the AFN sponsored the Indigenous Summit of the Americas[9] to create and promote a joint agenda to be presented to the Organization of American States (OAS) at their Summit of the Americas. In style and in substance, the Indigenous Summit acted as a government of a people, though without a state. A quick laundry list of concerns included: individual freedoms and rights and responsibilities, corporate responsibilities, environmental protection, intellectual rights, free trade, globalization effects, resource allocation, poverty eradication, education—in other words almost anything one might call his congressman or mayor about, save filling the local pothole.

Certainly there is no definitive cause and effect. According to Eric Zuelow of The Nationalism Project:

The nature of the internet is that one must go out to get information. "Push" technology never really got off the ground. Those who go searching for information about their own national community already are predisposed to nationalism. There are certainly internet-based communities, but I think you'd be hard pressed to call them nations. I have noticed that ex-patriot Scots (and Americans of Scottish heritage) tend to bond nicely on Scottish nationalism mailing lists. The catch here is that, as above, the members of the list are nationalists before joining the mailing list.[10]

Still, it is telling that this convergence of activity depends on the timely and accurate collection and dissemination of information—namely quasi-governmental endeavors—and parallels in time the maturation of a technology that transmits and enhances information flow almost effortlessly. There is also a telling convergence of the structure and purpose of such an organization as the AFN with the allegiance of its membership. Those that form and participate in such endeavors, based as they are on language and ethnicity, look to these structures to provide for certain services that are the traditional purview of governments—and may or may not be being met by the states in which they live. Arjun Appadurai writes:

> These disjunctions in the links among space, place, citizenship, and nationhood have several far-reaching implications. One of these is that territory and territoriality are increasingly the critical rationale of state legitimacy and state power, while ideas of nation seem increasingly driven by other discourses of loyalty and affiliation—sometimes linguistic, sometimes racial, sometimes religious, but *very rarely territorial*.[11]

In the case of the Indigenous Summit, one of the explicit prohibitions detailed was the intent not to alter the existing state structure or physical borders.[12] The tribes collectively have no desire to create or regain control of a physical state but want only to deal and be dealt with as a virtual state, as a legitimate representative organization of a people—even if by "people" it is meant "peoples," each with its own unique language and culture. No longer does a "nation" need a state to be accepted by its "citizens." Appadurai goes further; " . . . the territorial integrity that justifies states and the ethnic singularity that validates nations are increasingly hard to see as seamless aspects of each other."[13] A reawakened awareness of their native languages and culture, together with the impetus for political action to regain and maintain some control of their destiny as unique peoples, has been facilitated by the ease of information flow, storage, and retrieval through the Internet. Such impulses and desires as these were not created by the Net, but the obvious use of the Net to implement them speaks to a realignment of loyalties to communities not based on locality.

Membership in and even loyalty to Net-based communities does not necessarily come at the expense of citizenship in the political country of residency. To the extent that a virtual state or community offers or supplies support and services that are not available or are insufficient from the local or national government, such associations should lessen the aggregate need for such services upon the government. In like manner, the individual who uses the association to funnel his own efforts toward the "greater good" of his "brothers," however defined in the virtual nation, still provides part of the social "glue" upon which all society depends. Loyalties can overlap and run concurrently; an individual can be both a good citizen of his county and country and be active in his linguistic or cultural nation on the Net.

The other side of the coin, however, is when these separate loyalties come to cross-purposes or are in conflict. The leadership of either association may actively oppose the goals and aims of the other; indeed, if part of the reason for the creation of a virtual nation is the active discrimination of the members of the particular culture, then certainly the individual is faced with a stark choice. This is the case among many members of the global "nations" that increasingly embrace members living under the political rule of many individual countries.

Diasporas and the Net

Examples of nations pointing to definite points of origin or homelands are the Kurds of the Middle East and the Basque from their home in the Pyrenees. Both groups also have widely dispersed expatriate populations throughout the world, and both have resorted to violence to achieve a measure of political control of those homelands. Obviously, when there is territory that can be identified as "home," it still figures into the consciousness of nationhood. But the Internet may also affect how these peoples maintain ties and effect action.

> Politics is the struggle to determine the common interest of society and the struggle to dominate lawmaking and law-executing systems. There is no concept of the social unity of all humanity. Social and legal philosophy comes to a halt at national frontiers. Internet threatens traditional political institutions and perhaps even the very concept of sovereignty itself. The Internet permits political opposition groups to flourish more easily because of the decentralized nature of the Internet itself. Information technology has demolished time and distance which threatens the power structures of the world.[14]

No longer is it necessary to be "in place" to effect the politics and events in the homeland: The struggle to maintain a distinct identity can, and does, continue outside the control of the state. The stronger the identity maintained, and/or the greater the persecution of an identity, the greater the desire for political autonomy or self-determination.

As with indigenous groups, the cultural aspects of Basque and Kurd identity are being collected, disseminated, and preserved electronically on the Net. For example:

> The mandate of the Institute of Basque Studies is to promote and encourage research on the Basque language and culture, and to facilitate the dissemination of research material and publications for educational purposes. IBS was created in 1998, from the outset with a broad range of interests, and conceived to be an umbrella organization that co-ordinates and brings together scholars from a wide spectrum of areas of research in Basque studies.[15]

Again, many of these institutes and organizations do not predate the appearance of the web, and those that do have expanded to include a web presence. There may be something of a "build it and they will come" process at work: The numerous web sites, discussion rooms, personal pages, and newsgroups frequented by and designed for the Kurdish and Basque peoples reflect active and engaged populations who have found a medium that facilitates the maintenance of their unique identities.

Politically, the Basque region of Spain was awarded substantial autonomy in 1978—even to the extent that now the efforts of the European Union (EU) at coordinating tax structures are facing difficulty in accommodating Basque taxing modes.[16] But for so small a region, its official governmental web presence is detailed and expansive. Governmental services, points of contact, and information are all readily available. Political independence, and not just substantial political control, drive some elements of the Basque. There are those who strive for complete union of all the French and Spanish Basque regions, with concurrent independence from the host countries. Their fight is being waged in cyberspace with as much enthusiasm as in natural space: Information, disinformation, recruitment, and fundraising are all taking place on the Net, and accessed with ease.

> If it does not recover and secure its language and provides [sic] itself with the political instruments to govern itself and preserve its own identity, the Basque nation, assimilated by two powerful states, has the risk of

disappearing as such. To refuse to recognize the Basque right to self-determination is an attack against the Basque nation. Recognised or not, the right to self-determination is consubstantial to the recognition of equality among nations which comes from the democratic idea that sovereignty resides in the people and without any external interference. There is no better guarantee to peace and international collaboration.[17]

From Basque, one of the smallest regions for the battle of ethnic determinism, to Kurdistan, one of the largest, the political and cultural reasoning involved in the struggle are analogous:

Justice dictates that all nations are inherently equal and entitled to the same natural rights. That some nations are under the involuntary dominance of others presents an unnatural state and a source of imbalance in the lives of people and nations. In so much as voluntary unions are moral, legitimate and a source of prosperity and harmony, forced unions are immoral, illegitimate and harbingers of poverty and strife. Nations have the fundamental and natural right to determine the course of their own future. We, the Kurdish Nation, observing that all existing unions of the fragments of our Homeland with neighboring states are involuntary, and hence unnatural, immoral and illegitimate, declare them null and void. Whereas no nation seeks nor needs external consent to exercise its fundamental and natural right to self-determination, the Kurdish Nation likewise neither seeks nor needs any such alien consent in its exercise. For this and in order to preserve our pride and dignity, to revitalize and foster our customs and heritage, and to prevent the demise and dissolution of our identity, we the People of Kurdistan undertake to constitute an independent, unified and democratic state to include all of us within its body and to set us free to determine our own destiny. [18]

These fighting words, disseminated on the Net, refer to the centrality of language, culture, and people in the creation of a political presence. In the Basque case, physical boundaries remain important, but it is not the land per se that they seem to be fighting over—only the proposition that there needs to be a critical mass of acreage in which a threatened culture can maintain viability. In the case of the Kurds, the actual land area they can call a homeland is in no danger of assimilation, which frees the group to concentrate on the less tangible and more intrinsic qualities of nationhood—politics, linguistics, and culture.

In the Kurdish case, of course, a very concrete, territorially defined homeland transcends the political boundaries of present-day states.[19] However, the Kurds of each of these states are subject to different degrees of interference from their host governments—from subjugation to a measure of autonomy. Kurdish refugee and expatriate communities abound throughout the world, as do similar Basque communities, and they have also availed themselves of a presence on the web to promote and maintain cultural, linguistic, and political links. There is no recognized autonomous government in greater Kurdistan—but elements of one have been created in cyberspace. The American Society for Kurds, founded in 1997, is an NGO, and, with its website as one tool, helps to provide for and facilitate some traditional governmental services, namely health care, education, protection of human rights, and judicial and police training. Links to other quasi-governmental structures and political parties provide an indication of the depth of interest for the Kurds in some form of self-governance. Indeed, a Kurdish Parliament in Exile, founded in the Hague in 1995, exists primarily as an interest group, expounding in cyberspace on attempts to influence EU policy toward Turkey.[20] Even the Kurdish areas of Iraq that have become somewhat autonomous (liberated, in their term) have a functioning web presence, but those sites provide information only and are not designed to facilitate any services.[21]

The Greater the Effort

As the American Indians and other indigenous groups of the Americas found greater political clout by pooling their bodies and web sites at the Indigenous Summit, so too are nations otherwise unrepresented joining together as a true virtual "United Nations"—as distinct from the familiar one, composed of recognized nation-states. An ambitious effort, the Unrepresented Nations and Peoples Organization (UNPO) strives to fill this political void. From, of course, its web site UNPO defines itself:

> UNPO is an international organisation created by nations and peoples around the world, who are not represented as such in the world's principal international organisations, such as the United Nations.
> Founded in 1991, UNPO today consists of over 50 members who represent over 100 million persons. UNPO offers an international forum for occupied nations, indigenous peoples, minorities, and even oppressed majorities who currently struggle to regain their lost countries, preserve their cultural identities, protect their basic human and economic rights and safeguard the natural environment.[22]

Forums such as UNPO attempt to provide political clout, through collective engagement, to those peoples in danger of losing cultural identity. They boast as members such troubled nations in the news as the Acheh of Sumatra, the Chechen of Ichkeria, the Timorese of Indonesia, the Albanians of Kosovo, and the Kurds of, well, wherever they may be—as well as such quieter factions as the Assyrians of biblical fame, the Karenni of Burma, and the Tuva of Central Asia. One of the founding members of UNPO that has long been fighting for a restoration of political recognition is Taiwan. Counter to the principles now espoused through UNPO by Taipei, the native Taiwanese were long denied a voice by the nationalist Chinese upon their resettlement to the island after World War II. It is an interesting concurrence, and a possible lesson, that the awarding and acceptance of the rights of indigenous people by a host government—as finally occurred in Taiwan— may alleviate the violence often associated with the clash of cultures.

The creation and strengthening of umbrella organizations mirrors the strengthening of cultural identity. As a people assert or are awakened to their unique cultural or ethnic heritage and begin to demand a degree of political recognition and control based on such factors, the political landscape simultaneously undergoes both devolution and confederation stresses. The recent events in the British Isles vis-à-vis the EU illustrate the trend: Renewed Scottish political and cultural nationalism,[23] and a degree of political autonomy "devolved" to Edinburgh from London, meshes with and complements a similar degree of control "evolved" from London to Brussels and the EU. It is as if the center is being whittled away from both ends, and while the Internet did not cause such realignments, it has greatly facilitated the communication and education efforts necessary to achieve such political shifts.

Stateless Nations, Nationless States

This much is clear: hundreds of groups of people around the world who view themselves as connected due to language, culture, and/or point of origin have used the Internet to keep, maintain, and further that connectedness. The people involved no longer possess a physical home where their culture can grow, or their homeland is split and threatened by assimilation, or the land is distended and the people persecuted. Under such conditions, and others, the Net has become indispensable as the tool to maintain cultural and political cohesiveness. Conceivably, the Net may also be a strong factor in the creation of a cultural, linguistic, and political awareness. One's natural longing for connectedness may be stirred by a simple interest in the history of one's last name or a venture of discovery into roots.

Cyberspace, unlike its physical counterpart, is unique due to its potential limitlessness and unboundedness. On the Net, a nation's domain can be as large as desired or needed and can be accessed—or lived in—from anywhere. As cyber realms become more prevalent, more real, more interactive, more capable and responsive—indeed more self-organized as the number of online "citizens" approaches a critical mass[24]—there is a real risk of creating a certain displacement of loyalties to the created community on the Net. A community is what its members say it is, and when nations can stake out cyber territory and provide for services—political recognition, societal interaction, resource allocation, personal education—then the necessity for the same organized effort to deliver such services from state structures in real space could be affected.

The junctures between state and nation and cyberspace and real space are in a tremendous state of flux. Certainly the Palestinians, Basque, Kurds, Quebecois, Tibetans, and others who are fighting—politically or violently—for physical homelands will not be satisfied with realms limited to cyberspace. As long as distinct peoples are subjected to official or unofficial persecution or live under political regimes that fail to satisfy certain inalienable rights, the necessity for acreage will remain. However, when and if governments are or become more benign in nature or neutral to their aspirations, the need for land as a precondition for cultural survival may diminish. Indigenous peoples around the globe are laying claim to great swathes of cyber territory where they can live and thrive in peace—the implications of this trend for world politics are only beginning to be discovered.

Notes

1. For example, everything from the International Campaign to Ban Landmines (www.icbl.org) 1997, to the Congress of the National White People (www.nizkor.org) 1995, all with active web presence.

2. Indigenous Language Institute, accessed May 2001, http://www.indigenous-language.org.

3. Of the programs included, two-thirds have been in existence less than 15 years, and almost all less than 25. Indigenous Language Institute, accessed May 2001, http://www.indigenous-language.org/resources/directory/index.html.

4. Constable, Peter and Gary Simons, "Language Identification and IT: Addressing Problems of Linguistic Diversity," SIL International, SIL Electronic Working Papers, September 2000, http://www.sil.org/silewp/2000/001/SILEWP2000–001.html#1_intro.

5. Ibid., Sec. 1: Introduction.

6. For example: The Linguist List, http://linguistlist.org; Open Archives Initiative, http://www.openarchives.org; Terralingua, http://www.terralinga.org.

7. Assembly of First Nations, "History of the AFN: Assembly of First Nations—The Story," accessed May 2001, http://www.afn.ca/About%20AFN/history_of_the_afn.htm.

8. Assembly of First Nations, "Charter of the Assembly of First Nations: Preamble," accessed May 2001, http://www.afn.ca/About%20AFN/charter_of_the_assembly_of_first.htm.

9. Assembly of First Nations, "Indigenous Peoples Summit of the Americas," accessed May 2001, http://www.afn.ca/Summit/indigenous_summit_of_the_america.htm.

10. Zuelow, Eric, e-mail interview, March 2001, The Nationalism Project, Dept. of History, University of Wisconsin-Madison, http://www.wisc.edu/nationalism.

11. Appadurai, Arjun, "Sovereignty Without Territoriality: Notes for a Postnational Geography," in *The Geography of Identity*, ed. Patricia Yaeger (Ann Arbor: University of Michigan Press, 1996), p. 48.

12. Assembly of First Nations, "Towards a Principled Framework," sec. 3.3, AFN summit document, March 28, 2001, http://www.afn.ca/summit/edd/indigenous%20peoples%20summit%20of%20the%20americas%20%2D%20eng.doc.

13. Appadurai, "Sovereignty Without Territoriality," p. 57.

14. Zekos, Georgios, "Internet or Electronic Technology: A Threat to State Sovereignty," *The Journal of Information, Law and Technology*, sec. 3, October 29, 1999, http://elj.warwick.ac.uk/jilt/99–3/zekos.html.

15. Institute of Basque Studies, "IBS: Introduction," accessed May 2001, http://ibs.lgu.ac.uk/ibshome/page1.html.

16. Bourn, Angela, "The EU's 16th Member State in Taxation Matters? The Basque Taxation Regime, the Challenge and the Defence," First International Symposium on Basque Cultural Studies, Institute of Basque Studies, London Guildhall University, June 29, 2000, http://ibs.lgu.ac.uk/sympo/ANGEL.PDF.

17. Astrain, Luis Nunez, "A Pending Matter of Self-Determination," excerpted from "La Rason Vasca," editorial in the periodical *Txalaparta*, 1995, http://www.contrast.org/mirrors/ehj/html/frself.html.

18. Kurdish Worldwide Resources, "The Kurdish Manifesto," 1997, http://www.kurdish.com/kurdistan/legal/manifesto.htm.

19. Turkey, Iraq, Iran, and Syria

20. Agira, accessed May 2001, http://www.ariga.com/kurdish.htm.

21. Kurdistan Regional Government, accessed May 2001, http://www.krg.org.

22. Unrepresented Nations and Peoples Organization, Main Page, accessed May 2001, http://www.unpo.org.

23. Aided, no doubt, by Hollywood's Scottish nationalist portrayals in the films *Braveheart* and *Rob Roy,* both released in 1995.

24. A concept explored by Mitchell Waldrop in *Complexity: The Emerging Science at the Edge of Order and Chaos* (New York: Simon and Schuster, 1993).

CHAPTER 3

Come Together?
Debunking the Myth of the Internet and the Global Village

Emil T. Bailey, Jr.

There is much talk these days about the creation of a "global village," largely due to the rapid spread of telecommunication and information technology, particularly the Internet. In a recent series of interviews conducted by *Internet Magazine,* many of the world's Internet and technology gurus speculated on what effect they believe the Internet will have in the decades ahead.[1] Common responses were that the Internet "has an incredible power to bring people from all walks of life together" and that "it breaks down barriers between people and countries, creating a true global village." This telling oxymoron has become ubiquitous, but far more people use the phrase than ask whether it is true.

The feature in *Internet Magazine* quoted Bill Gates's book, *The Road Ahead,* which states that "The Internet will draw us together, if that's what we choose, or let us scatter ourselves into a million communities." The stronger case exists for the latter idea. There is and will be no global village; at least not in the sense that the phrase is commonly used. The Internet is not bringing us together but is helping to strengthen parochial identities. Several facts and trends support this conclusion, beginning with the unavoidable fact that most of the world's population remains outside the Internet's reach. Furthermore, those that are connected to the Internet are largely using the technology for more recreational and functional purposes, as opposed to broadening their understanding of, and contact with, other cultures of the world. Some are even employing the Internet for nefarious rather than unifying purposes. Indeed, the belief that the Internet will create a global village may, in fact, have terrible repercussions.

Measuring Levels of Connectivity

According to a study on the world's Internet population by CommerceNet, in January 2000 there was a total of 242 million people connected to the Internet.[2] The vast majority of these people, 120 million, were in the United States and Canada, and of that number, more than 83.3 million were in the United States (as of April 1999). Projections for future growth suggested that by 2002 the world's Internet population would have grown to at least 490 million, with 165 million of that number being in the United States. In second place for the January 2000 figures was Europe, with 70 million users. It is of little surprise that these regions would rank the highest, given their advanced levels of economic and technological development, and it is also a small surprise that the comparative numbers in other regions, especially the developing world, are vastly smaller: In Asia there are 40 million people online, in Latin America 8 million, and in Africa 2.1 million.

But the picture is even more segregated than that. Tables 3.1 and 3.2, derived from figures given by the CommerceNet study, provide a more detailed picture of the patterns of Internet connectivity in the Asian and Latin American regions, making clear the vast gulfs between the more and less advanced countries within them.

As these tables show, the more economically advanced a country is, the greater its Internet population. Although the information from CommerceNet is somewhat dated, as it was compiled in 1999, more recent figures from the Intellibridge Corporation, an Internet consult-

Table 3.1: Asia

Country	Internet Population	Percentage of Total Population
Australia	4.2 million	32
China	1.5 million	0.1
Bangladesh	7,000	.005
Hong Kong	850,000	13.4
India	800,000	.08
Indonesia	80,000	.04
Japan	14 million	13.4
Malaysia	600,000	3
New Zealand	561,000	15.8
Philippines	200,000-320,000	0.3-0.4
Singapore	510,000	17
South Korea	3.5 million	7.8
Sri Lanka	14,000	.07
Taiwan	3.01 million	14.3
Thailand	131,000	0.2
Vietnam	11,000	.014

Source: http://www.commerce.net/research/stats/analysis/WWInternetPopul-Asia.pdf

ing firm in Washington, DC, while showing a few differences from the CommerceNet numbers, reflect the same pattern. In terms of connectivity in Asia, the Intellibridge report notes that:

> the Web remains out of reach for many Asians . . . Internet users are concentrated in a few, mainly developed, countries and regions . . . Australia, Japan, Hong Kong, Singapore, and South Korea. Many Southeast and South Asian markets lack the necessary Internet and telecoms infrastructure to support mass-scale usage of the Internet . . . The cost of purchasing a personal computer is a major impediment to growth.[3]

Both the CommerceNet[4] and Intellibridge[5] studies for Latin America and Africa point out that insufficient infrastructures are significant barriers in these regions as well. The CommerceNet analysis of South

Table 3.2: Latin America

Country	Internet Population	Percentage of Total Population
Argentina	250,000	0.65
Bolivia	8,000	0.11
Brazil	3.5 million	2.1
Chile	150,000	1
Colombia	350,000	.95
Costa Rica	30,000	*
Dominican Republic	25,000	*
Haiti	2,000	*
Mexico	600,000	0.6
Paraguay	1,000	.01
Peru	20,000	.08
Uruguay	90,000	2.7
Venezuela	80,000	3.3

* Percentage of population data not available
Source: http://www.commerce.net/research/stats/analysis/WWInternetPopul-SAmerica.pdf

America adds the challenge of connection costs. Citing a 1997 report from the Organization for Economic Cooperation and Development, CommerceNet states that the average monthly cost for Internet access in Mexico, one of Latin America's largest Internet populations, was $95.[6] This is prohibitive in a country where nearly half the population subsists on $100 a month.[7] It is no surprise that 90 percent of Latin America's Internet users were from upper-middle and high socioeconomic classes. Another author on the Internet and Latin America adds that these individuals are "primarily urban, male, white, [and] middle-aged."[8]

The disparities in connectivity are even more striking elsewhere, as the Intellibridge study on Africa's connectivity pointedly states:

To get an idea of how unwired Sub-Saharan Africa is, consider the fact that there are currently a little over 1.5 million Internet users in the entire region, with over 1million of those users located in South Africa, leaving roughly 500,000 amongst the remaining 734 million people on the continent. That means one Internet user for every 1,500 people.[9]

Martin Hall, in his article "Africa Connected," adds:

> There are . . . two dimensions to Africa's connectivity. At the larger scale there are major disparities between South Africa and the rest of the continent . . . Within South Africa, there are huge contrasts between the urban, largely white and increasingly commercial users of information and communications technology, and rural, overwhelmingly African, communities who have only partial access to basic telecommunications.[10]

The global pattern, then, is mirrored at the regional level, and again within countries. It becomes difficult to argue that the Internet is creating a global village when so much of the world's population remains locked outside of its gates, barred from participating by the high costs of entry related to building infrastructure, purchasing equipment, and paying for access. Rather, the Internet merely reflects the existing gaps between the world's rich and poor, as is mirrored by the even larger gap in what might be called the "information rich" and "information poor."

Some proponents of a rapidly emerging global village suggest that wireless Internet capabilities and the decreasing costs of technology will help bridge this gap. That may someday be true, although the numbers make an exceptional case for not expecting true global connectivity in our lifetime or even the next. Even if the gap is somehow bridged, there is no reason that this should create a global village, particularly given the trends of current Internet usage. A close examination of the surfing patterns within countries reveals trends that are not conducive to bringing people of differing social, religious, and economic backgrounds together and creating greater understanding. If anything, current trends in usage suggest that the Internet is serving best as a mechanism of bringing together elements disaffected by globalization, as opposed to creating any globalized elite who could serve as the foundation for a global village.

How the Internet Is Used

Perhaps it is best to begin with how the Internet is being used in the United States, since it is the most wired country in the world. If the

Internet is creating a global village, it must be particularly doing so where its presence is greatest, and this, then, ought to be reflected in how the Internet is being used in such regions. In November 2000, the Center for Communication Policy at UCLA released its first annual Internet report, "Surveying the Digital Future."[11] The report explores the effect the Internet has on social, political, cultural, and economic behaviors, attitudes, and ideas among users and nonusers. The findings of the report raise many questions about the idea that the Internet is creating a global village.

According to the study, the top ten most popular Internet activities are outlined in Table 3.3 (see below). The trend is clear: The Internet is being used largely as a recreational tool rather than an instrument to broaden one's horizons and reach out to other cultures around the world to celebrate the newfound global village. Indeed, when the breakdown of activities is given in terms of time spent in hours per week online according to gender, the number one activity for both males and females over the age of 18 is listed as "Entertainment: Games, Hobbies, etc." at 43.3 and 43.0 percent respectively.[12] Similarly, males and females ages 12 to 17 also devoted most of their time online to "Entertainment: Games, Hobbies, etc."[13]

Also noteworthy is that, even in the United States, Internet demographics reflect those of the world in general, with the richer part of society being far more wired. Some 88.6 percent of people with incomes ranging from $100,000 to $149,999 are Internet users while 87.3 percent with incomes greater than $150,000 are users.[14] This contrasts with the 41 percent of those earning less than $15,000, and 61.5 percent of those earning $15,000 to $49,999.

The specific browsing patterns of different income groups bring the picture of division into even starker relief: Internet users with more experience online spend a greater amount of time looking for news, trading stocks, and making investments; those with less experience tend to play games and pursue hobbies. The Nielsen/NetRatings group, which provides extensive services in measuring Internet audiences, examined audience behavior in June 2000 and found that those in lower income brackets and with less education mostly visited entertainment sites such as ICQ.com, WalMart.com, Emazing.com, Wotch.com, and SendingFun.com while those in higher income brackets and with more education visited web sites such as Schwab.com, Boston.com (the Boston Globe's web site), TheStreet.com, CNBC.com, and MajorLeagueBaseball.com.[15]

Conspicuously absent from this picture are web sites promoting other cultures and greater understanding. Although some may attempt

Table 3.3

Top Ten Most Popular Internet Activities	Percent of Users
1. Web surfing or browsing	81.7
2. E-mail	81.6
3. Finding hobby information	57.2
4. Reading news	56.6
5. Finding entertainment information	54.3
6. Buying online	50.7
7. Finding travel information	45.8
8. Using instant messaging	39.6
9. Finding medical information	36.6
10. Playing games	33.0

Source: http://www.ccp.ucla.edu/UCLA-Internet-Report-2000.pdf, p. 10.

to argue that trips to news web sites and chat rooms could lead to such exposure, it is doubtful that such information is being accessed. It is more likely that these people are seeking information related to their broader surfing patterns.

However, proponents of the global village may contend that people of differing backgrounds are brought together by similar surfing patterns. Some argue that the Internet creates "communities of concern" that help break down geographical and cultural barriers, as people sharing similar interests can come together online, thus increasing their contacts with, and exposure to, one another.[16] These communities of concern unite members with diverse interests and backgrounds who also happen to share one particular interest, and this fosters friendships and understanding between Jews and Gentiles, blacks and whites, and dozens of other divided groups.

The data about actual Internet usage make this position radically unpersuasive. Not only are Americans spending their time online entertaining and trying to enrich themselves materially rather than understanding others, but these activities are largely segregated by social factors created in the real world and imposed on the virtual world. Besides, of course, there is no guarantee that virtual contact will somehow alter the real world preconceptions people take with them into the cyberworld. A racist may have a heartfelt conversation with someone else online, unaware that they are of another race, and then go out in the real world and continue to view the members of the other race in the same light as before. Also, even if cordial contact is made while ethnicity or religion remains anonymous, once such factors are revealed, there is nothing that says individuals will not react according to their prejudices toward such groups. It is important to stress the fact that racial and other such characteristics must ultimately be revealed; after all, greater understanding and tolerance cannot be fostered unless someone is aware that they are communicating with someone of another ethnicity or religion.

But even granting that online interactions between people of different countries, cultures, and economic classes could foster greater understanding and tolerance, this is certainly not transpiring on a large scale in the United States, as the UCLA internet report's data on online friendships and e-mail shows. Only a little more than one-quarter (26.2 percent) of Internet users say they have online friends they have never met, and these users averaged slightly more than a dozen (12.9) such friends, while only 12.4 percent of users said they met someone online whom they have since met in person, and averaged 5.6 such new friendships.[17] It is important to note that the report did not indicate if any of these new friendships involved individuals of different ethnic, economic, or religious backgrounds, nor did the report offer any insight into the geographical proximity of these individuals.

The report's findings on e-mail usage also do not support the notion that the Internet is creating a global village. The study uses a scale from 1 (greatly decreased), to 3 (stayed the same), to 5 (greatly increased) to gauge if the Internet has increased the number of people users regularly stayed in contact with.[18] The average response was 3.3, showing little change. When Internet users were asked specifically if they were communicating with friends and family more since they started using the Internet, the average response was again 3.3. Similarly, there was little change noted when subjects were asked if the Internet had decreased the level of contact. When asked if it is easier to meet people online rather than in person, with response options being 1 (strongly disagree) to 5 (strongly agree), the average response was 2.5.

The responses in this section are enlightening in several ways. First, contact with family and friends showed no great increase or decrease due to the Internet. This makes sense, since most of these relationships are facilitated through the geographical proximity most people have to those in this category, as would be the case with professional colleagues. Those relationships showing the most positive enhancement by the Internet (although be it rather meager) are relationships based on kinship, geographical proximity, frequent interaction in the real world, shared experiences, interests, and, it's a safe bet to say, language—

exactly the sort of relationships that would stiffen existing segregation and divisions rather than ease them.

The Internet and Culture

This brings us to one of the most significant misconceptions about the Internet and the global village: the idea that the Internet is culturally diverse. The reality is that the Internet is heavily culturally skewed. Even with the growth of non-native English speakers, English continues to be the dominant language, accounting for 70 to 80 percent of the Internet's content.[19] Although this may not be a problem to many of the elite in the world—as exemplified by one study that found that 80 percent of Internet users in Latin America did not see English as an obstacle[20]—it is definitely a hindrance to the many poor people in the developing world, who can not even read or write their own language, much less English. There is no reason, however, to expect English's domination to continue. Nevertheless, this does not mean progress in the direction of the global village, as Intellibridge's Asia analysis states:

> English is not the native language of 70 percent of Internet users. Most prefer to navigate the Web in their native language . . . the number of Internet users in the [People's Republic of China] [will reach] 300 million by 2005. The PRC is expected to overtake the U.S. as the country with the most Internet users before then. And many of these users will be checking out Chinese-language sites. Instead of facilitating communication and understanding among people, the Internet could make things worse.[21]

Thus, the Internet will likely become segregated according to language, and unless a person speaks the language of a particular group, he or she will be cut off from communicating with that group. The result will be to reinforce group identities rather than give rise to any concept of a global identity.

The Internet's ability to reinforce the "village" at the expense of the "global" becomes especially clear in light of the common uses by groups in the developing world. Cultural Survival, a think tank dedicated to the needs of the world's indigenous populations, conducted a series of studies on the Internet's impact on indigenous cultures around the world, which provides telling insight into this phenomenon.[22] There are repeated accounts of how indigenous groups (ranging from the Maya in Guatemala, tribes in the Amazon, ethnic minorities in Burma, the Sami of Scandinavia, the scattered Assyrians, and the Oneida of

New York state) have used the Internet to reinforce and reinvigorate their sense of "indigenousness." The groups used the Internet as a storehouse for language, culture, customs, and history, and they used e-mail to create networks for distributing news about the issues facing these groups, usually to scattered diasporas. As one section comments, "With greater use of the Internet by indigenous peoples, ethnic identities became much more important. People who did not formally belong to an indigenous group rediscovered their ethnic heritage."[23] The result, as one of Cultural Survival's reports dealing with the Internet's impact on native cultures in Canada's Northwest Territories notes, is that "Like tribes, virtual communities maintain coherent group identities and resist assimilating into a larger society."[24]

Yet this assessment is not without debate. This particular section of Cultural Survival's survey catalogues the opinions of the members of various tribes who are the most active online in their respective communities—and their opinions differ markedly. Fred Lepine, of the Metis, sees the Internet as capable of dismantling even strong cultures but bases this assumption on an analogy to television.[25] An excellent rebuttal to this comes from Jim Bell, a member of the Inuktitut, who does not believe the Internet will wipe out his culture, saying that as opposed to television, the Internet provides a means of "fighting back."[26] James Hrynyshyn, a member of the Yellowknife, affirms the point, arguing that the Internet's capability to carry audio, visual, and text transmissions makes it ideally suited to the storytelling traditions of indigenous cultures.[27]

The overwhelming theme of the article, despite the concerns voiced, is that the Internet will help strengthen local identities, even if there is a tradeoff with some aspects of any emerging "global culture." This attitude is replicated elsewhere in the developing world. Soraj Hongladrarom, who studies the Internet's impact on Thai culture, observes that "local cultures usually find ways to cope with the impact and are resilient enough to absorb it without losing some kind of identity."[28] In explaining how local cultures co-opt the Internet, he says:

> [The Internet] acts like a universal conduit, carrying ideas and information from one place to another. Since the global and the local are negotiated, locals have a leeway to consider and pick only those aspects carried by the universal conduit for their use. If they find ideas . . . to their liking, then they will consider adopting them. They will debate among themselves whether these ideas should be adopted at all, or how much they should be modified to suit the local scene before they are adopted and taken as part of the local cultures.[29]

Demonstrating how this can result in an end product completely different from what the concept is understood to be in its point of origin, Hongladrarom gives the example of American sympathy for Czech demonstrators demanding "truth and justice." In fact, he suggests, if the two parties sat down and discussed what the meanings of "truth and justice" are, they would find themselves in disagreement.[30]

Perhaps even more powerful evidence supporting this metamorphosis is seen in Islam's relationship with the Internet. A recent report about Muslim women who have adopted the Purdah, or secluded lifestyle, illustrates the way in which the local is morphing the supposed global more than other way around.[31] Some Muslim women in the Purdah system have turned to the Internet to access the outside world—not to be drawn into a global village but to reinforce their separate lifestyle. Many of the women who participated in Muslim chat rooms expressed the happiness that Purdah brings, and the conversations focused more on where to find more comfortable face covers than on the restrictions the women live under. Also, as more and more Muslims enter cyberspace, the article says that Islamic scholars are trying to develop codes for proper online behavior, asserting that real world rules are just as applicable in the cyberworld. Some women have already voluntarily adopted these rules, such as indicating that they are veiled when logging on to a chat room. Furthermore, given that women's role in public life under the Purdah system is limited to begin with, the ability to do online shopping and other activities over the Internet could greatly diminish the reasons these Muslim women have to leave the house. As a consequence, the idea of the freedom the Internet brings could be altered to such an extent that most people in the West, and especially the United States, would hardly recognize it.

The Consequences

The argument that the Internet serves as the engine of a global village falls into the trap of technological determinism, which, as Philip Agre writes, is the idea that technology has an independent effect on society, entirely determined by the technology itself.[32] Agre helpfully reminds us that detailed empirical studies show something else entirely: The direction technology takes is not inevitable and is shaped in important ways by societal forces. The Internet will be used only in ways that people can imagine and that fit in with their existing system of beliefs and relationships. Accordingly, the Internet may amplify existing forces, but it will be difficult at best to determine whether it has any independent force of its own.

This amplification process, as Agre points out, can have positive or negative results. Illustrating a positive aspect, the Internet is frequently cited, for example, as being a key component in the international campaign to band land mines.[33] From her home in Vermont, Jody Williams used the Internet to organize a coalition of 1,300 NGOs allied to ban the production, storage, and use of landmines in most countries. But one need not look far to find an equally, and perhaps even more powerful, negative consequence of this amplification effect. Testifying before the Senate Select Committee on Intelligence, Director of Central Intelligence, George Tenet, warned:

> Usama bin Laden and his global network . . . remain the most immediate and serious threat . . . At the same time, Islamic militancy is expanding, and the worldwide pool of potential recruits for terrorist networks is growing . . . [these] networks have used the explosion in information technology to advance their capabilities. The same technologies that allow individual consumers in the United States to search out and buy books in Australia or India also enable terrorists to raise money, spread their dogma, find recruits, and plan operations far afield. Some groups are acquiring rudimentary cyberattack tools. Terrorist groups are actively searching the Internet to acquire information and capabilities for chemical, biological, radiological, and even nuclear attacks.[34]

Echoing the severity of this threat is General Mike Hayden, the director of the National Security Agency (NSA), who has commented that the NSA is struggling to keep up with the global telecommunications revolution that provides terrorists such as bin Laden a vast communications infrastructure.[35] The NSA was monitoring the communications of bin Laden as he was preparing the attacks on the U.S. embassies in Africa in 1998, but the agency was unable to collect enough intelligence to stop it. The extent of this threat was made painfully apparent by the events of September 11, 2001, which illustrate the degree to which modern day terrorists have been empowered.

Even at a lesser extreme, the breakneck pace at which the Internet is being pushed to cultures as part of an effort to construct a global village can have adverse and counterproductive results, such as reviving and reinforcing local identities and animosities. An account of a web site for Nigerian immigrants to the West, dubbed Niajanet, explains how the internal divisions present in Nigerian society were not only carried over to new countries but were also transplanted "even in an idealized, or 'virtual' space . . . "[36] The author notes that as a result of disagreements over language, local politics, and other issues, a number of subsidiary web sites were erected based on the various ethnic identities of Niajanet users.[37] This would follow the broader trend in regard to virtual communities, showing that they tend to be monolingual and homogenous.[38] It should be kept in mind that this was the impact with a small number of Nigerians from among the more educated and wealthy of their society; what can we expect when the Internet is made available to the wider Nigerian society? In all likelihood, we can expect an even more pronounced trend toward strengthening ethnic identity and language. This must be taken in the context of compelling arguments that English plays a crucial role in holding together Nigerian society, which is composed of more than 300 distinct ethnic groups, each with its own language.[39]

There is some evidence that Synchronous Automated Translation Systems (SATS), which operate on artificial intelligence and provide instantaneous translations, may help the Internet break down language barriers by allowing individuals to communicate in their native tongue in virtually all mediums and have their words precisely translated into many other languages.[40] Even so, it hardly follows that the technology will independently alter the prejudice, hatreds, and perceived slights one group holds toward another. Even those praising SATS caution that the technology may actually exacerbate problems between cultures, especially in regard to assimilating diasporas, resulting in greater linguistic fragmentation and political turmoil.

Another problem with introducing the Internet into troubled regions of the world is that it could be used as a means of disseminating false information in an effort to ignite hostilities. This has already been seen in Malaysia, where shortly after deadly clashes between ethnic Malays and Indians erupted an e-mail alleging the unrest was continuing was circulated with the intent of reigniting the clashes.[41] An excellent analogy for the potential repercussions lies in the example of Rwanda, where a single mobile radio broadcasting from the back of a Toyota pickup truck was used to encourage the genocide in the African country.[42] What could be achieved with the Internet needs to be conceived not only in the context of its reach but the apparent trust given to information received from the Internet. According the UCLA report, 54.7 percent of Internet users believe most or all information on the Internet is reliable.[43] Of even more concern, as one source states in regard to the Internet's ability to spread rumors, "With contrived images and manipulated pictures, things are unlikely to improve."[44]

Another possible drawback could be that the Internet becomes a mistaken panacea for the developing world's problems. As one indigenous person put it, "Our village does not have running water. Why should we have running data?"[45] When the Internet arrives with great fanfare—and concrete progress in the standard of living remains elusive—the result may be to rehash unsettled animosities. As the following passage illustrates, the Internet is already being used as a tool in the saga of indigenous peoples' struggle against inequity:

> [Indigenous peoples] were able to exchange information pertaining to a continental saga set within the framework of the nation-state, globalization, and human rights. People started to build exchanges and organized meetings with the purpose of furthering decolonization. Indigenous collective entities continued to struggle for the preservation of their livelihoods and territories against the reckless incursion of transnational corporations. For indigenous peoples, the debate was, and still is the struggle over colonialism, neocolonialism, and liberation.[46]

Thus, the Internet may end up generating greater discontent than harmony in the developing world. Imagine how members of an indigenous tribe will feel once they go online and find the stock value of the oil company plundering and polluting their tribal lands: a stock valued at a price they will most likely not be able to afford, a stock whose value has come from the wrecking of their homeland. One might hope that the Internet will create greater awareness of their plight, but users in the developed world seem inclined to use the Internet to entertain themselves or are more concerned about whether or not the oil company's stock is a good buy. Conversely, users in the developing world seem intent on employing the technology to strengthen rather than loosen local, cultural, and traditional ties, as well as their sense of injustice. Such effects could have serious consequences for stability in the developing world. The National Intelligence Council, in assessing future threats to U.S. and international security, has commented that:

> Traditional communal groups-whether religious or ethnic-linguistic groups-will pose a range of challenges for governance. Using opportunities afforded by globalization and the opening of civil society, communal groups will be better positioned to mobilize coreligionists or ethnic kin to assert their interests or defend against perceived economic or political

discrimination. Ethnic diasporas and coreligionists abroad will also be more able and willing to provide fraternal groups with political, financial, and other support.[47]

There is nothing ignoble about the hope embodied in the idea of the global village, but much more caution and prudence must be exercised in the euphoric rush to bring the Internet to the rest of the world. More attention should first be given to alleviating other factors in the developing world, particularly in regard to structural reforms aimed at creating greater pluralism and more equitable distributions of wealth. Interjecting the Internet into these regions with the misconception that it brings people together and leads to greater understanding will likely create false hope and rising expectations that will go unfulfilled. The reaction to this could be disastrous for the stability of the developing world, triggering more civil wars, state fragmentation, and ethnic cleansing—quite the opposite of what one would expect in a global village.

Notes

1. "It's Your Future!" *Internet Magazine* (August 1, 2000): p. 54.
2. CommerceNet, Industry Statistics, Worldwide Internet Population, January 2000, http://www.commerce.net/research/stats/wwstats.html.
3. Intellibridge Corporation, Global Scenarios Brief, "Wired Societies: How the Internet Is Transforming Business in Asia," February 2001, p. 4, par. 1, http://www.intellibridge.com/briefbook/pdf/wired_societies.pdf.
4. Jeremy Lieb, "Worldwide Internet Population: South America," CommerceNet, *Newsletter, Facts, Figures, and Forecasts* 1, no. 5 (May 1999), http://www.commerce.net/research/stats/analysis/WWInternetPopul-SAmerica.pdf; Jeremy Lieb, "Worldwide Internet Population: Africa," CommerceNet, *Newsletter, Facts, Figures, and Forecasts* 1, no. 7 (July 1999), http://www.commerce.net/research/stats/analysis/WWInternetPopul-Africa.pdf.
5. Intellibridge Corporation, Global Scenarios Brief, "Latin America," November 1999, http://www.intellibridge.com/briefbook/pdf/latin_america.pdf; Intellibridge Corporation, Global Scenarios Brief, "Africa and the Middle East," June 2000, http://www.intellibridge.com/briefbook/pdf/africa_mideast.pdf.
6. Jeremy Lieb, "Worldwide Internet Population: South America," p. 1, par. 4, http://www.commerce.net/research/stats/analysis/WWInternetPopul-SAmerica.pdf.
7. Fernando Rodriguez-Alvez, "Present and Future of the Internet in Latin America: A Tile Research Report," Trends in Latin American Networking (TILAN) Project, University of Texas, June 1999, par. 5, http://lanic.utexas.edu/project/tilan/reports/Present&Future.html.
8. Ricardo Gomez, "The Hall of Mirrors: The Internet in Latin America," *Current History* 99, no. 634 (2000): 72; also available at The International Development Research Centre, par. 6, http://www.idrc.ca/pan/pubhall_e.htm.

9. Intellibridge, Global Scenarios, "Africa," p. 1, par. 2.
10. Martin Hall, "Africa Connected," *First Monday* 13, no.11, (November 2, 1998): par. 10, http://www.firstmonday.dk/issues/issue3_11/hall/index.html.
11. University of California at Los Angeles (UCLA), Center for Communication Policy, "The UCLA Internet Report: Surveying the Digital Future," November 2000, http://www.ccp.ucla.edu/UCLA-Internet-Report-2000.pdf.
12. Ibid.
13. Ibid., p. 14.
14. Ibid., p. 12.
15. Nielsen/NetRatings, "Less Well To-Do Web Surfers Spend More Time Online Than More Affluent People, According to Nielsen/NetRatings," September 21, 2000, tables 1, 2, 3, and 4, http://www.nielsen-netratings.com/pr/pr_000921.htm.
16. Jim Mann, "Communities of Concern Will Change Our World," *The Futurist* (May/June 2001): 68–69.
17. UCLA, "The UCLA Internet Report," p. 34.
18. Ibid.
19. Gomez, "Hall of Mirrors," par. 3.
20. TILAN Project, "Present and Future," par. 3.
21. Intellibridge Corporation, "Wired Societies," p. 4, pars. 4.
22. "The Internet and Indigenous Groups," *Cultural Survival Quarterly* 221, no. 4 (winter 1998), http://www.cs.org/publications/CSQ/csqinternet.html.
23. Guillermo Delgado-P. and Marc Becker, "Latin America: The Internet and Indigenous Texts," *Cultural Survival Quarterly* 221, no. 4 (winter 1998): par. 10, http://www.cs.org/publications/CSQ/csqinternet.html#Becker.
24. Barry Zellen, "Surf's Up!: NWT's Indigenous Communities Await a Tidal Wave of Electronic Information," *Cultural Survival Quarterly* 221, no. 4 (winter 1998): pars. 9, http://www.cs.org/publications/CSQ/csqinternet.html#Zellen.
25. Ibid., par. 17.
26. Ibid., par. 16.
27. Ibid., par. 9.
28. Soraj Hongladrarom, "Negotiating the Global and the Local: How Thai Culture Co-opts the Internet," *First Monday* 5, no. 8 (August 2000): par. 3, www.firstmonday.dk/issues/issue5_8/hongladarom/.
29. Ibid., par. 25.
30. Ibid., par. 22.
31. Sofia McFarland, "Living in Purdah: Muslim Women Bond on the Net," Dow Jones News Service, 5 April, 2001.
32. Philip Agre, "The Dynamics of Policy in a Networked World," draft paper, October 19, 1999, pars. 4–5, http://dlis.gseis.ucla.edu/people/pagre/policy.html.
33. Robert A. Rastor, ed., *A Century's Journey: How the Great Powers Shape the World* (New York: Basic Books, 1999), p. 16.
34. George Tenet, director of central intelligence, "The Worldwide Threat 2001: National Security in a Changing World," testimony before the Senate Select Committee on Intelligence, February 7, 2001, pars. 6, 9, 10, http://www.cia.gov/cia/public_affairs/speeches/UNCLASWWT_02072001.html.
35. General Mike Hayden, interviewed on *60 Minutes II,* CBS, February 13, 2001.
36. Misty Bastian, "Nationalism in a Virtual Space: Immigrant Nigerians on the Internet," *West Africa Review* 1, no. 1 (July 1999): 13, par. 3, http://www.westafricareview.com/war/vol1.1/bastian.pdf.
37. Ibid., pp. 4–9.

38. Hall, "Africa Connected," par. 19.

39. Ted Anthony, "English in Action: People and a Language, Changing Each Other," Associated Press Newswires, April 16, 2001.

40. Sam Lehman-Wilzig, "Babbling Our Way to a New Babel: Erasing the Language Barriers," *The Futurist* (May/June 2001): 16–23.

41. Tony Emmanuel and Lee Shi-Ian, "Police Also Prepare to Detain Author of E-mail Containing Rumors," *The New Straits Times,* 23 March 2001.

42. James Adams, *The Next World War: Computers Are the Weapons and the Front Line Is Everywhere* (New York: Simon and Schuster, 1998), pp. 272–274.

43. UCLA, "The UCLA Internet Report," p. 22.

44. Frank James, "Web Users See 2 Sides to the Coin Called Internet, Survey Finds," *Chicago Tribune,* 26 October 2000.

45. Steve Cisler, "Introduction: The Internet and Indigenous Groups," *Cultural Survival Quarterly* 221, no. 4 (winter 1998): par. 7, http://www.cs.org/publications/CSQ/csqinternet.html#Cisler.

46. Delgado-P. and Becker, "Latin America," par. 11.

47. The National Intelligence Council, "Global Trends 2015: A Dialogue about the Future with Nongovernment Experts," December 2000, p. 41. Also available at par. 1, http://www.cia.gov/nic/pubs/2015_files/2015.htm#link11c.

CHAPTER 4

Subnational Groups and the Internet: An Irritant to Globalization, Not a Threat

Tania Stanley O'Neil[1]

In 1994, the Zapatista National Liberation Movement and Army (EZLN) undertook a campaign of harassment and low-intensity military operations against the government of Mexico. The movement, based in Chiapas, has been described variously as an insurgency and as a social movement against international neoliberalism. The Zapatistas have used the Internet to counter the characterization of its organization put forward by the Mexican government, to link itself to international supporters, and to attempt to stimulate global resistance to neoliberalism and globalization. In their use of technology, the Zapatistas are one example of a new and revolutionary model for organization in the current global age.

A key question is whether backlash groups such as the Zapatistas can make effective use of the Internet to counter or threaten the emerging global system. One potential implication posed by the rise of the Internet and technological interconnectivity—a force that cannot be controlled by any one government—is a shift away from the known international order. Analysis of the Zapatista case study enhances the understanding of the risks of subnational groups working against the established international order across state borders. And yet, while the Zapatista Internet presence is an interesting phenomenon, it demonstrates the limits of the technology as well as its utility. Even a group successful in its use of the Internet to support its cause, the Zapatista example seems to suggest, will end up using the medium primarily for traditional communication tasks and will not be able to garner enough momentum online to achieve what it could not otherwise achieve— stalling the movement toward globalization.

The Zapatista Movement

The Zapatista National Liberation Movement and Army emerged into global consciousness on January 1, 1994, when the armed wing seized control of four towns in Chiapas, Mexico. The movement had been in development by the late 1980s and early 1990s.[2] According to Bishop Samuel Ruiz, who served for a time as a mediator between the Zapatistas and the Mexican government, Mexican government forces began destroying guerilla training camps and training grounds in Chiapas over the course of 1993, so the emergence of armed conflict between the movement and the Mexican government was not a complete surprise.[3]

The Zapatistas have traditionally presented themselves as a decentralized organization with no single person in charge. The nominal leader of the movement uses the pseudonym Subcommander Marcos; he is widely considered the leader of the movement, despite the fact that he generally has claimed that no one person leads the Zapatistas. Both organizational and military decisions are allegedly "left to the Revolutionary Indigenous Clandestine Committee-General Command (CCRI-CG of the EZLN). This body is made up of community elders from the Zapatista controlled territory. But even this body is not the final authority behind the EZLN. All major political decisions are made by community assemblies."[4] However, in a March 2001 interview with Colombian novelist Gabriel Garcia Marquez, Subcommander Marcos admitted that he was the military leader of the Zapatistas.[5] Another leader later became apparent during the Zapatista address to Mexico's Congress in March 2001, identifying herself as Commander Esther, the leader of the Zapatista's civilian movement.[6]

The movement has experienced mixed results since its inception. After the initial, brief conflict (lasting about two weeks), the movement and government engaged in dialogue for most of 1994.[7] Following the inauguration of the Institutional Revolutionary Party (PRI) candidate Ernest Zedillo as Mexico's president near the end of 1994, Mexican government forces renewed their effort to quell the Zapatista insurgency.[8] The Zapatistas found themselves in retreat until they managed to renew dialogue with the government in mid-1995.[9] Both sides eventually agreed to the San Andres Accords in February 1996, which were intended to improve the condition of Mexico's indigenous population.[10] After agreeing to the accords, the Zapatistas seemed to rely more heavily on unarmed marches and protests to demonstrate in favor of their cause for a period of time.[11] However, President Zedillo did not seriously pursue the San Andres Accords. From 1996 through the end of Zedillo's term at the end of 2000, both Mexican government forces and Zapatista forces stand accused of conducting intermittent armed raids and other purposeful armed harassment against each other.[12] Nonetheless, the Zapatista movement has been remarkably nonviolent and has relied primarily on words as its weapons.[13]

The Zapatista movement has yet to build momentum since the PRI was voted out of the Mexican presidency in 2000, and it does not seem poised to do so. Mexican president Vicente Fox's tendency toward inclusivity and willingness to listen to the Zapatistas may be removing the grounds for rebellion from the traditionally anticentral government movement. Fox took office in December 2000 and, as one of his first acts, ordered Mexican government forces in Chiapas to return to barracks in Chiapas.[14] In March 2001, the Mexican government removed military forces from the last of seven bases according to the demands of the Zapatistas.[15] In March 2001, the Zapatistas conducted a march into Mexico City and addressed Mexico's Congress to lobby for an indigenous people's rights bill (based on the 1996 San Andres Accords). The march was allowed—even welcomed by Fox's presidential radio address—and the Zapatista bus caravan that traveled from Chiapas to the Mexico City area was protected by Mexican federal police at least some of the time.[16] The Fox government has subsequently offered a series of agreements to the Zapatistas, and while the movement has rejected them—on the grounds that they contain inadequate benefits for the indigenous population—the dialogue seems certain to continue.[17]

The nature of the Zapatista movement itself is in transition. In a March 2001 interview with Gabriel Garcia Marquez, Subcommander

Marcos admitted that the Zapatistas no longer seek armed conflict.[18] "If the Zapatista National Liberation Army continues as an armed force," Marcos admitted, "it is destined for failure."[19] The Zapatistas apparently believe that their successful address to the Mexican Congress transformed them from an insurgency into a political force.[20] President Fox reportedly views the Zapatista movement and his own ascendancy to the presidency as proof that democracy has arrived for Mexico.[21]

The Zapatista Agenda

The Zapatistas launched their rebellion on January 1, 1994, to coincide with the implementation of the North American Free Trade Agreement (NAFTA), because they believed NAFTA to be a "death sentence" for Mexico's poor.[22] They also are against the Free Trade Agreement of the Americas (FTAA). Upon their emergence in January 1994, the Zapatistas issued a declaration of war based in part on Article 34 of Mexico's constitution, which says: "National Sovereignty essentially and originally resides in the people. All political power emanates from the people and its purpose is to help the people. The people have, at all times, the inalienable right to alter or modify their form of government."[23] The domestic agenda of the Zapatistas is anti-PRI and anti-sexism, and is geared toward self-determination for all peoples—especially Mexico's indigenous population—and preservation of the environment.[24] Based on a Zapatista document, "Declaration from the Lacandon Jungle" demands also include: "work, land, shelter, food, health, education, independence, freedom, democracy, justice, and peace."[25] Subcommander Marcos has repeatedly stated that the Zapatistas do not seek political rule over Mexico.

By January 1996, the Zapatistas had broadened the scope of their movement beyond the concern for the Mexican indigenous and poor population to include concerns about international globalization and neoliberalism. The Zapatistas claim to fight globalization, neoliberalism, and the moneyed powers of multinational corporations, which they believe remove power from the local area and increase the poverty of the poor. They seem to equate globalization, the concept of increased integration of capital, technology, and information across national borders and the ascendancy of the power of free markets over governments, with neoliberalism, a term they define as free market capitalist economics.[26] They believe that NAFTA is a "keystone of neoliberalism on the American continent."[27] They also consider "neo-liberalism as a system implemented by the seven most developed countries of the world and accepted by the previous Mexican government [Zedillo and the PRI], [and think it] has served as a henchman of imperialism."[28]

The Zapatistas apparently came to believe in the need to fight "global neoliberalism" as one segment of a larger transnational community. Around April 1996, they hosted "The Continental Forum on Behalf of Humanity and against Neoliberalism" in Chiapas, Mexico. This event drew 400 scholars and activists from the United States, Europe, and ten Latin American states, and "strategies for taking the offensive against the domination of free market policies were examined."[29] In July and August 1996, the Zapatistas hosted the First Intercontinental Encounter for Humanity and against Neoliberalism. The event was also held in Chiapas, Mexico, and about 3,000 activists from 43 countries attended, according to a sympathetic website.[30] At the end of this event, Subcommander Marcos delivered closing remarks during which he called for the Intercontinental Consultation for Humanity and against Neoliberalism in December 1996 and for the Second Intercontinental Encounter for Humanity and against Neoliberalism to be held on the European continent in the second half of 1997.[31]

Enthusiasm for the First Intercontinental Encounter for Humanity and against Neoliberalism apparently did not persist. The Zapatistas sent only two delegates to the Second Intercontinental Encounter for Humanity and against Neoliberalism.[32] It was held in Spain in July and August of 1997, and organizers claim 3,000 people from 50 countries attended.[33] At the conclusion of the second encounter, there was a call to change the meeting schedule of future encounters from an annual to a biannual basis. Of note, there is no mention of additional transnational encounter-type meetings in the electronic Zapatista community or in electronic encounter indexes. It appears the Spain 1997 encounter was the last of its kind.

The Zapatistas and the Internet

The Zapatista movement has made use of technology and the Internet since its inception, and in so doing has been hailed by some as a new, revolutionary model for organization in the post–cold war global age. The Zapatistas, several assessments have concluded, represent "one of the most successful examples of the use of computer communications by grassroots social movements."[34] Recent visits to the Zapatista web site show that it is conscientiously maintained, as it is consistently current within weeks.[35] In 1998, the Zapatistas were identified by *Wired* magazine as "one of the twenty-five most important people online."[36]

The Zapatistas have used the Internet to organize, communicate, and counter Mexican government propaganda. There is an entire Zapatista community beyond the movement based in Mexico that exists electronically and that is comprised of groups sympathetic to the Zapatista cause.[37] The Zapatistas have "created a distribution network of information with about 100 or more autonomous nodes of support."[38] Subcommander Marcos reportedly has used a laptop computer to issue orders to EZLN units and to prepare and post his communiqué documents to communicate the Zapatista movement philosophy and message to Mexico and the world.[39] He also reportedly communicates directly with foreign media contacts to "maintain a favorable international propaganda image," particularly at times in the past when the Mexican government has issued anti-Zapatista propaganda.[40]

The Zapatistas also have used the Internet in negative ways to conduct deception or disinformation campaigns and computer network attacks. In fact, the Zapatista protest style on the Internet led to the phrase "digital Zapatismo." Zapatista deception tactics have involved using the Internet to claim military movements or violence by Mexican government forces that eventually were proven untrue.[41]

On at least two occasions, the Zapatistas have been involved in computer network attacks. The Zapatistas collaborated with the Electronic Disturbance Theater (EDT) in September 1998 to conduct a 10,000 person virtual sit-in against Mexican president Zedillo, the U.S. Pentagon, and the Frankfurt Stock Exchange.[42] The attack delivered 600,000 hits per minute to each site and was considered a success by EDT. When the Pentagon sensed the attack, it responded with "a counter-offensive against the users' browsers, redirecting them to a page with an Applet program called 'Hostile Applet.' Once there, the Applet was downloaded to their browsers, where it endlessly tied up their machines trying to reload a document until the machines were rebooted."[43] Zedillo reportedly did not respond to the September attack but did respond to a June 1998 attack by forcing user computers to open windows endlessly until they crashed. The Frankfurt Stock Exchange admitted it knew of the protest but "believed it had not affected . . . services."[44] The relationship between Zapatista and EDT leadership is unclear, but EDT publicly stated that its reason for engaging in this activity was to garner more attention for the Zapatista movement.

Assessment of the Zapatista Movement

Despite the Zapatista movement's successful use of technology as a fundamental component of its work, it is a movement that likely will either sputter along as a Mexican government irritant or be assimilated within Mexican political discourse. The Zapatistas have not gained momentum in recent years, and their theoretical foundation has become increasingly weak. The Zapatista movement has become more of a spent force; it undercuts itself by criticizing the globalized system that has produced the transnational technologies the movement uses and that has the potential to produce benefits for Mexico's indigenous people, such as employment.

The Zapatistas are unlikely to gain renewed momentum for their movement, as they are becoming increasingly mainstream. Following a dramatic start in 1994, the Zapatistas quickly found themselves in a stalemate with the Mexican government. They relied primarily on physical and verbal protests and electronic demonstrations to vocalize the Zapatista cause throughout much of their history. Events of March 2001—when the Zapatistas were welcomed into Mexico City and granted an audience at the Mexican Congress—did much to highlight the fact that the foundations of an insurgent Zapatista movement are increasingly shaky. The movement that claimed collective or decentralized leadership for seven years finally admitted that it does have individuals that serve as military and civil leaders. The movement that vigorously opposed the PRI and former president Zedillo now lacks the force to rally against the current government and, in fact, faces an accommodating Mexican government leadership in the form of President Fox. The San Andres Accords of 1996 that the Zapatistas fought so hard to achieve in order to improve the situation of Mexico's indigenous population served as the basis for legislation submitted to Mexico's congress by President Fox after he took office in December 2000. Once significant legislation for the Mexican indigenous population is achieved, it could be argued that the Zapatistas will have the bulk of the reasons for their existence removed. President Fox has complied with a number of Zapatista demands since his inauguration, including ordering Mexican force removal from seven bases identified by the Zapatistas and releasing a number of jailed persons identified by the Zapatistas. In the face of a more accommodating Mexican government, the stubbornness of the Zapatistas appears anachronistic.

On the international side, the Zapatista campaign against globalization and neoliberalism contains contradictions. The Zapatistas consider globalization to be a negative force, yet the movement makes use of the very benefits provided by globalization when it uses the Internet to communicate across state lines and encourage transnational interest in the Zapatista cause. Likewise, the Zapatistas criticize globalization as a force that increases poverty and do not admit that globalization actually can increase the number of jobs available to Mexicans—which is one of the Zapatista's key demands.

Assessment of Zapatista Use of the Internet

For the most part, the Zapatistas have relied on the Internet as a tool to communicate with the outside world. The Internet remains an ineffective method to communicate with the Zapatista's own domestic constituency, the majority of which do not have Internet access. "The Zapatista communities are indigenous, poor and often cut-off from not only computer communications but from the electricity and telephone systems through which the former mostly operate."[45] The Zapatistas continue to have an international electronic community. In fact, an ambitious idea was suggested at the Second Intercontinental Encounter for Humanity and against Neoliberalism in Spain in 1997. This proposal suggested a "network of struggles and communication" be established[46]:

> By network we understand a movement under permanent construction of people and organizations interconnected among themselves that will link, communicate and coordinate the different struggles of prevention, resistance and action for Humanity and against Neoliberalism. Made up of organized entities, individual or collective, interrelated among themselves, without a specific center, with a horizontal structure, that send and receive information and are capable of organizing themselves for the undertaking of common acts, using all technological means available and all forms of social relations. As the Second Declaration of La Realidad says: "The net is all of us who talk and listen . . . all of us who resist. With local, supralocal, national and international levels until we build the Planetary Net for Humanity and against Neoliberalism."[47]

There is no evidence that the idea for a network for humanity and against neoliberalism saw fruition. If so, the Zapatistas appear to have no link to such a network. Presumably, this idea went the way of additional encounter meetings discussed above. However, the international electronic Zapatista community does persist through such groups as the Irish Mexico Group.

Most of all, the case seems to demonstrate that the Internet cannot change fundamental political facts. The Zapatista movement has an uncertain future because of broad political trends and realities in Mexico; unless that fact changes, no amount of global attention to the Zapatista web presence will boost its fortunes. It is likely that the movement attained greater international attention than would have been the case without the Internet, and that this contributed to the perceived need by the Mexican government to engage in dialogue. Even this conclusion, though, cannot be strongly supported. In the pre-Internet age, a figure as charismatic and media savvy as Subcommander Marcos would have used telephones and radios and leaflets and visits to international media outlets to get his message out, and the effect might have been largely the same.

Subnational Backlash Groups and the Internet: A Threat to the Global System?

The Zapatistas are one so-called backlash group that reacted negatively to the current global system by having an international aspect to their movement specifically directed against globalization. The question is raised as to whether such a subnational group networked to others transnationally could damage the international order. One theory, suggested by Charles Swett of the U.S. Office of the Assistant Secretary of Defense for Special Operations and Low-Intensity Conflict (Policy Planning), is that a group making use of the Internet could possibly be afforded a reactive speed and "degree of influence that is disproportionately strong relative to their actual numbers."[48]

While the Zapatista movement demonstrates an interesting phenomenon in its use of the Internet, however, this case indicates that, even through successful use of the Internet, subnational groups cannot significantly alter the overall global system, or even the progress of globalization within their countries, unless other political, economic, and social factors are arrayed in support of its cause. (The irony, of course, is palpable. A subnational group that makes use of the technological byproducts of globalization such as the ability to organize electronically across state borders is only able to do so thanks to globalization, and it works through the very system it decries.) The Zapatista movement's use of the Internet has not measurably increased the threat it poses to the Mexican government.

Studies of other cases of Internet use for similar purposes have come to the same conclusions. Dr. Michael Dartnell of York University, Canada, has undertaken a research project called "Insurgency Online" under a research grant from the U.S. Institute of Peace. Dartnell is examining Internet use by antigovernment political movements, and the Zapatistas are among the groups monitored.[49] The project is particularly interested in the implications of transnational insurgent political movements for the international system and democratic development.[50] One of his major efforts has looked at the Peruvian insurgency, Movimiento Revolucionario Tupac Amaru (MRTA), and he concludes that online insurgencies "do not alone constitute [a] threat to state power . . . but [do] in some sense dramatically alter political communication."[51] In other words, the Internet simply provides another way to communicate and does not pose a threat to the global order in and of itself.

The Zapatista movement has made impressive use of the Internet since its emergence in 1994. However, the significance of the Internet for the movement has been primarily in the realm of communications rather than in the realm of insurgency. The future of the Zapatistas in Mexico is uncertain, and the movement's past involvement in larger transnational antiglobalization efforts appears to have died out. The Zapatista case is corroborated by the Peruvian MRTA case. One of Dr. Dartnell's conclusions for the MRTA is also fitting for the Zapatista movement: "Overall, the effect of IT [information technology] is less to overwhelm states than to become part of the 'global village' phenomenon . . . In other words, the Internet is another context in which politics occur, issues are generated and specific conditions pertain."[52] The Zapatista movement has always been an irritant, not a substantial threat, to the Mexican government and the existing global order, and it appears that the Internet did not change that status at all.

Notes

1. Ms. O'Neil has worked as an analyst for the Department of Defense since 1995 and resides in Arlington, Virginia. The views expressed in this paper are those of the author and do not reflect the position or policy of the Department of Defense or the U.S. government.

2. Harry Cleaver, "The Zapatista Effect: The Internet and the Rise of an Alternative Political Fabric," *Ciberlegenda* no. 3 (2000). Posted February 19, 2001 on http://www.uff.br/mestcii/cleaver.htm.

3. Sergio Munoz, "Interview: Samuel Ruiz Mediating for Peace and Social Justice in Chiapas, Mexico," *Los Angeles Times*, 10 May 1998. Posted on May 5, 2001, on http://flag.blackened.net/revolt/mexico/comment/ruiz_interview.html.

4. Jason Wehling, "Zapatismo: What the EZLN Is Fighting For," *The University Sentinel*, 10 January 1995. Posted February 21, 2001, on http://flag.blackened.net/revolt/mexico/comment/why.html.

5. Associated Press, "Zapatista Leader Rejects Warfare," *The Washington Post*, 25 March 2001, p. 25.

6. Ginger Thompson and Tim Weiner, "Zapatista Leaders Make Their Case to Mexico's Congress," *The New York Times*, 29 March 2001, p. A4.

7. Munoz, "Interview." "Toward a History of Events in Chiapas," posted February 21, 2001, on the Irish Mexico Group home page, http://flag.blackened.net/revolt/mexico/ralertdx.html.

8. Ibid.

9. Ibid.

10. Rosalva Bermudez Ballin, trans., "San Andres Accords," posted May 5, 2001, on the Irish Mexico Group home page, http://flag.blackened.net/revolt/mexico/ezln/san_andres.html. Javier Elorriaga, "The Significance of the San Andres Agreements to Civil Society," posted May 5, 2001, on the Irish Mexico Group home page, http://flag.blackened.net/revolt/mexico/comment/sig_san_andres.html.

11. "Toward a History of Events in Chiapas," February 21, 2001.

12. Ibid.

13. Ginger Thompson and Tim Weiner, "Zapatista Rebels Rally in Mexico City," *The New York Times*, 12 March 2001, p. A7.

14. "Toward a History of Events in Chiapas," February 21, 2001.

15. "Toward a History of Events in Chiapas," posted May 5, 2001, on the Irish Mexico Group home page, http://flag.blackened.net/revolt/mexico/ralertdx.html.

16. Associated Press, "Zapatistas March Into Mexico City," *The New York Times*, 11 March 2001. Posted March 11, 2001, on http://www.nytimes.com/aponline/world/AP-Mexico-Rebels.html.

17. "Toward a History of Events in Chiapas," May 5, 2001.

18. Associated Press, "Zapatista Leader Rejects Warfare."

19. Ibid.

20. Thompson and Weiner, "Zapatista Leaders Make Their Case to Mexico's Congress."

21. Associated Press, "Zapatistas March Into Mexico City."

22. Wehling, "Zapatismo: What the EZLN Is Fighting For."

23. "First Declaration from the Lacandon Jungle. EZLN's Declaration of War 'Today We Say Enough Is Enough! (Ya Basta!),'" posted May 5, 2001, on the Irish Mexico Group home page, http://flag.blackened.net/revolt/mexico/ezln/ezlnwa.html.

24. Wehling, "Zapatismo: What the EZLN Is Fighting for."

25. Ibid.

26. Thomas Friedman's definition of globalization is quoted in Robert S. Litwak, *Rogue States and U.S. Foreign Policy: Containment after the Cold War* (Baltimore, MD: Johns Hopkins University Press, 2000), p. 253.

27. "The Gatherings for Humanity and against Neoliberalism," posted February 21, 2001, on http://www.geocities.com/CapitolHill/3849/gatherdx.html.

28. Irish Mexico Group Newsgroup, "From Quebec to Acteal, Chiapas: Resistance to Oppression of Globalization," 20 April 2001, e-mail newsletter.

29. "Zapatista Conclave a Reality Check for Neo-liberalism," posted May 5, 2001, on http://geocities.com/CapitolHill/3849/rossla.html.

30. "The Gatherings for Humanity and against Neoliberalism," February 21, 2001.

31. "Closing Words of the EZLN at the Intercontinental Encounter—Second Declaration of La Realidad for Humanity and against Neoliberalism," posted May 5, 2001, on http://www.geocities.com/CapitolHill/3849/dec2real.html.

32. Cecilia Rodriguez, "The Sounds of Silence and the Zapatistas," posted May 6, 2001, on http://www.utexas.edu/students.nave/.

33. "Zapatistas in Cyberspace," posted February 21, 2001, on http://www.eco.utexas.edu/Homepages/Faculty/Cleaver/zapsincyber.html#Analyses. "The Second Intercontinental Gathering for Humanity and against Neoliberalism," posted May 6, 2001, on http://www.utexas.edu/students/nave/.

34. "Zapatistas in Cyberspace," February 21, 2001.

35. View the official EZLN website in Spanish at http://www.ezln.org/.

36. Dorothy Denning, "Activism, Hacktivism, and Cyberterrorism: The Internet as a Tool for Influencing Foreign Policy," posted March 19, 2001, http://www.nautilus.org/info-policy/workshop/papers/denning.html.

37. View http://www.eco.utexas.edu/Homepages/Faculty/Cleaver/zapsincyber.html#Analyses for a sampling of this community.

38. Denning, "Activism, Hacktivism, and Cyberterrorism."

39. Charles Swett, "Strategic Assessment: The Internet," posted February 19, 2001, on the Federation of American Scientists home page, http://www.fas.org/cp/swett.html.

40. Swett, "Strategic Assessment." Cleaver, "The Zapatista Effect."

41. Swett, "Strategic Assessment."

42. Denning, "Activism, Hacktivism, and Cyberterrorism."

43. Ibid.

44. Ibid.

45. Cleaver, "The Zapatista Effect."

46. "Final Declaration of the 2nd Encounter for Humanity and against Neoliberalism in Spain, July 1997," posted May 6, 2001, http://www.pangeo.org/encuentro/.

47. Ibid.

48. Swett, "Strategic Assessment."

49. See project mission statement at http://www.yorku.ca/research/ionline/mission.html.

50. "Curriculum Vitae—Dr. Michael Dartnell," posted March 14, 2001, on http://www.yorku.ca/research/ionline/cv.html.

51. Michael Dartnell, "Insurgency Online: Elements for a Theory of Anti-government Internet Communications," Small Wars and Insurgencies 10 (winter 1999): 116.

52. Ibid., p. 128.

CHAPTER 5

The International Security Implications of Internet Use Via Satellite

Glenn Hickok

The Internet was originally designed in the late 1960s to decentralize military communications and thereby make the U.S. military less vulnerable in the event of global conflict. Subsequently, it became a tool for major research and academic institutions to exchange scientific data. Eventually, providing the general populace access to rapid data transfer at a reasonable cost enabled the Internet's expansion into the commercial sector. Only after a large base of users was established did the network truly achieve the impact that is evident in society today. Currently, the United States is the predominant user of the Internet, with approximately 75 percent of a recently estimated worldwide total of 200 million users.[1] This percentage is forecast to shift dramatically over the next five years: By 2005, 75 percent of a predicted 1 billion users will reside *outside* of the United States.[2]

These projections, which mirror trends toward a more globalized marketplace, have been widely discussed, but the national security

ramifications of widespread dependence on the technology that provides Internet connectivity is often overlooked. Spreading the reach of
the Internet is a laudable goal, but inherent weaknesses in connectivity
have the potential to decrease international stability and may make the
U.S. military more vulnerable.

The demand for bandwidth to satisfy growing communication over
the Internet has several potential solutions, including increasing traditional terrestrial phone line infrastructure, cable modems and digital
subscriber lines (DSL), fiber optic cables, and communication via
satellite. The last option, accessing the Internet from satellite transmissions, offers many advantages. These include operation where traditional phone lines do not exist, the ability to provide service to a
wide swath of the planet from a central location, and efficient point-to-
multipoint distribution that is conducive to on-demand applications.[3]
Satellite communication capabilities are particularly appealing to developing nations that don't currently posses the communications
infrastructure already established in more industrialized nations. However, utilization of satellites to disseminate information creates a central
transmission point for all data, offering a lucrative target to potential
adversaries. Developing nations (and rural areas in the developed
world) will surely benefit from the competitive advantages provided by
satellite-based Internet access, but in the long run a system dependent
on satellites will be more vulnerable to numerous forms of mali-
cious attack.

The Internet's Importance

As the Internet has emerged in the mainstream as a global form of
communication, it has taken on an increasingly important role in a
nation's overall health, especially in the economic realm. This linkage
can be attributed to the increased role of the Internet in global commerce, national infrastructure, and facilitation of both personal and
institutional intellectual pursuits. These notions are now taken for
granted, but to fully understand how the Internet can make society
potentially vulnerable, it is important to remind ourselves of the details.

Global commerce is an important element of a nation's economy
because it enhances financial stability and promotes sustainable development.[4] It is an increasingly important mechanism for job and wealth
creation.[5] The capabilities of the Internet offer expanded opportunities
in international trade and enable more efficient domestic business
practices. Not only has the Internet become a tool to increase business

potential and efficiencies, but it has become a practical necessity in order to compete at almost all levels of commerce. With Internet traffic growing at over 100 percent annually,[6] electronic commerce transactions are expected to reach $3 trillion by 2004.[7] Fueling most of this growth will be projected increases in business-to-business and business-to-consumer e-commerce of 300 percent and 125 percent respectively from 1998 to 2003.[8]

Perhaps even more important than e-commerce is the broad array of business-to-business applications now resident on the Internet, including supply-chain management and aggregated markets. Through the establishment of such online tools, national infrastructures are becoming dependent on the Internet. Increasingly, the public sector is embracing similar tools to enhance efficiency, bringing them even further into the everyday aspects of personal life. Critical infrastructures such as electrical grids, phone networks, banking and finance, physical distribution, and vital human services of advanced nations are increasingly software driven and remotely managed and maintained through computer networks.[9] The technology provided by the Internet expedites operations and reduces manpower, allowing re-allocation of fiscal resources to other sectors, further facilitating growth. However, while this electronic-based architecture allows for an efficient use of limited resources, it also leads to chokepoints for vital information distribution.

The Internet is also of importance because it accelerates the accumulation of a nation's intellectual capital—a more qualitative, but perhaps ultimately more important, effect of the technology. By allowing connectivity to other domestic and international research institutions, intellectual pursuits are accelerated and subjected to additional scrutiny before grassroots research turns into more fiscally demanding product development. The Internet also allows access to a plethora of learning tools for primary and secondary education. Additionally, individual awareness and choice is enhanced through access to boundless sources of information previously limited by physical constraints.

The Internet's utility and importance have translated into growth. Merrill Lynch estimates that the number of people around the world accessing the Internet over a variety of connections will likely increase to 1.4 billion by the end of 2009, compared to 200 million at the end of 1999.[10] Commensurate with this expanded use is an increase in the means by which data is transported, generically referred to as "bandwidth," the amount of data that can be sent over a relay at any given time. While existing telephone bandwidth is ample for voice communication, the dramatic increase in relaying computer-generated data over the Internet will over-inundate the existing global telecommunications

infrastructure over the next several years.[11] Figure 5.1 illustrates how a
once ample commodity suddenly becomes scarce when faced with a
global abundance of computers generating data at a rate of gigabits per
second, and how the projected demand grows enormously over the next
four years.

It is this growth that creates the context for the policy dilemma facing
the United States. Demand for bandwidth is exploding, along with e-
commerce, software applications, and intellectual exchange, which
increasingly underpin the fabric of the U.S. economy. The Internet must
adapt to the growing demand yet remain sensitive to future vulnerabilities
that may emerge.

Meeting the Demand for Bandwidth

Exploding global bandwidth requirements are projected to overwhelm
most existing telecommunication infrastructures. Three alternatives
offer solutions to the current dilemma: Fiber optics, cable/digital
subscriber lines, and Internet connectivity via satellite linkage.

Fiber optic cables, one avenue to compensate for the excessive
demand, are long, thin strands of very pure glass about the diameter of a
human hair, bundled into cables to transmit light signal over long
distances.[12] These cables have enormous capacity to transmit large
amounts of broadband data. Current cables from Alcatel, a leading
developer of optic capability, had in 2001 the capacity to carry 420
Gigabits/sec (Gb/s) on a single fiber, a figure likely to grow to 680 Gb/s
in the near future.[13] Once in place, these cables significantly reduce the
cost of Internet transmissions when compared to copper cables.[14]
Much like the copper transoceanic cables that exist for overseas
communication today, fiber optic cables will reside on the ocean floor
to provide Internet connectivity to different continents.

Another way to provide Internet connectivity and satisfy increased
bandwidth demands would be through DSL and cable modems. DSL
provides high-speed Internet access over a single dedicated telephone
line, while cable modems provide access over a shared cable television
line.[15] These technologies can increase bandwidth up to 7 Megabits/s
(Mb/s) incoming and 1 Mb/s outgoing.[16] While both fiber optics and
DSL/cable modems can serve to mitigate the problem of bandwidth
supply exceeding demand, they also require sizable financial commit-
ments to develop the required infrastructure, an alternative many
developing nations may not find appealing or realistic in the near term.

Figure 5.1

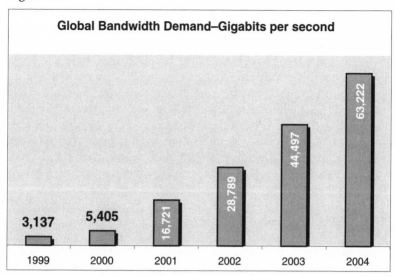

Source: Fishburn, *The World in 2001*[17]

Relaying Internet data via satellite is a third option, and in many ways the most attractive. This method of transmission enables Internet access without the geographic restriction of high-speed terrestrial lines. While technology is emerging to conduct these transmissions over mobile phone networks to satellite constellations in low-earth orbit (LEO), the predominant practice is to utilize satellites in Geosynchronous earth-orbit (GEO) with fixed ground units, called very small aperture terminals (VSATs).[18] VSATs, commonly used for services such as ATM transactions, credit card authorizations, and real-time inventory control, offer the advantage of communicating with one satellite that covers a large portion of the earth's surface and have become more technologically mature over the past decade.[19]

For a number of reasons, satellites stand out as the most likely answer to the world's rising need for bandwidth. Satellite technology lends itself to users not easily serviced around the world; it is ideal for areas unable to develop and sustain large telecommunication infrastructures. Once a satellite is launched, it can serve millions via a few ground stations.[20] Cost efficiency is another advantage: Satellites avoid the expense and difficulty of laying fiber in geographic areas with rough terrain and to sparsely populated areas.[21] Satellites also provide simultaneous access, which allows satellite companies to reach many customers at once, regardless of distance or geography.[22] The ubiquity of such a system also enables users to adopt a single high-speed platform for an entire continent and provides the world with one service provider and one bill.

These advantages have led satellite broadband providers to target those economies where terrestrial telecommunications infrastructure is underdeveloped. Industry forecasters are also optimistic about the expanded role satellites may play in more developed regions, where it is uneconomic to provide broadband data terrestrial solutions.[23] Demand will only increase as cost, driven by mass-market terminal production and low prices for high-end performance, declines. Overall, the broadband data sector for satellites is expected to generate over $18 billion in revenue by 2007.[24]

Satellite broadband systems will therefore be counted upon to bring the benefits of high-speed access to users in rural and remote areas that have no other access to high-speed telecom facilities, such as cable modems or DSL. This concept has the strong financial backing of numerous companies both within the United States and abroad. In particular, countries in South Asia and the Middle East see this path as the most efficient way to meet communication needs. Two companies will provide satellite service for these regions. Asian Cellular Satellite Service (ACeS) is already on contract to provide services to Indonesia, the Philippines, and Taiwan and is licensed to start service in India in mid-2001. Similarly, Thuraya, based in the Middle East, has already signed agreements with Etisalat in UAE, Qatar Telecon in Qutar, PTCL in Pakistan, Sudatel in Sudan, and GPTC in Libya (others are expected to follow suit).[25]

The capabilities and business strategies of both these companies are fostering increased use of satellite technology for Internet connectivity in these regions. Both ACeS and Thuraya offer satellite service with wide footprints that provide the coverage required for business and individuals to capitalize on Internet technologies.[26] They have also cooperated in close conjunction with regional governments through a business plan that espouses a partnership between their services and the existing national infrastructures. The philosophy of electing to complement rather than compete with national operators is allowing telecommunication companies to extend their access in developing the markets and augment existing Internet services.[27]

In the United States, with its strong existing infrastructure and widespread access to phone or cable lines, the picture is more mixed. The number of small business and home offices demanding satellite services is expected to grow in the short term,[28] in part to solve the "last mile" problem in some areas where DSL or cable capabilities for Internet access do not reach to individual homes.[29] However, by 2006 terrestrial broadband connections are expected to exceed demand, and some analyses project that satellites will begin to lose their share of the Internet and communications market.[30] The United States will most likely proceed with fiber optics to satisfy the majority of its increased bandwidth requirement in the long term (past 2006), because a significant portion of the required commercial terrestrial infrastructure is in place and fiber optic transmission costs are lower than satellite costs.[31] Fiber also offers the advantages of longevity (25 years expected line life versus 10 to 15 years for a satellite), no transmission delay, security (from intercept and missiles), ease of repair, and greater capacity.[32] There will be a satellite market for rural users in the United States, but the predominant portion of the population will most likely be served by fiber optics or other landline technologies.

Western Europe, on the other hand, is significantly undersupplied by terrestrial broadband infrastructure.[33] As a result, satellites can capture a larger market share for a longer period of time in that area.[34] However, as figure 5.2 indicates, a large amount of the communication between Europe and North America can be supported using fiber optic cable laid on the ocean floor.

While figure 5.2 emphasizes the point that thickly trafficked routes requiring low latency will favor fiber optic solutions, the required infrastructure to accomplish this, outside of North America, is not likely to materialize in the near term, if at all.

Despite the U.S. trend toward fiber, several factors bode well for increased global use of satellites over the next decade. First, as mentioned before, electronic commerce transactions are expected to reach $3 trillion by 2004. With the majority of Internet growth coming from outside the United States, a significant demand in satellite-based broadband services is likely.[35] Merrill Lynch, in the report *Global Satellite Marketplace 2001,* underlines this argument with several facts:

- Rising demand for broadband data services via satellite will drive growth in the satellite industry.
- The inability of global land-based wireline and wireless connectivity alternatives to keep pace with demand for high-speed, bandwidth-on-demand data communications bodes well for the satellite sector.
- The satellites industry's inherent advantage lends itself to serving those users not easily served around the world.

Figure 5.2

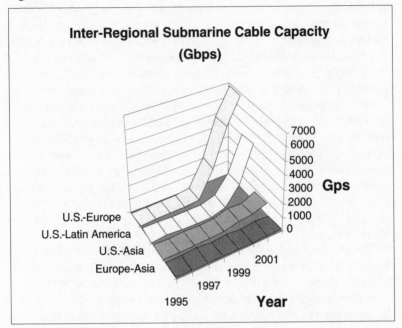

- While the first generation Ku-band two-way high-speed data service will be somewhat slower than terrestrial broadband alternatives, this service will do especially well where users will never have access to ground-based high-speed Internet service.[36]

The above factors, in conjunction with a 1997 World Trade Organization (WTO) agreement on making expansion of satellite services in a competitive market a priority,[37] make a convincing argument that nations responsible for the largest amount of Internet growth over the coming decade will become increasingly reliant on satellites.

The Vulnerability of Satellites

While attractive for economic and infrastructure reasons, satellite-based Internet connectivity creates new national security vulnerabilities. This is true because satellites are very delicate and vulnerable pieces of equipment, subject to a wide range of possible attacks. Potential kinds of attack include disruption activities that temporarily deny access to space-derived products, physical attacks that completely destroy a satellite system (the ground station, launch systems, or satellites in orbit), and actions with the potential to render space useless for human purposes over an extended period of time.[38]

High-energy laser weapons are ideal for harassing satellites because they are capable of producing intense, damaging beams of optical radiation. This radiation can be used to permanently damage a satellite by overheating it and possibly melting or tearing the satellite's "skin" with a hammer-like mechanical impulse, generated on a target's surface.[39] Because the origin of such an attack is much more difficult to trace than an attack by other means, use of directed energy from a laser weapon also offers plausible deniability for the perpetrator if the attack is successful.[40]

Kinetic energy attacks, such as the use of an electromagnetic pulse (EMP), could also be used to disable satellites. An EMP, commonly associated with nuclear detonation but achievable through conventional means by employing microwave technology,[41] can be characterized as a very short (nanoseconds) but intense electromagnetic pulse. The shockwave creates an extremely powerful field of energy that results in a large transient voltage (thousands of volts) exposed on electrical conductors (wires) and circuit boards. Damage from this energy on electrical equipment is devastating and irreversible.[42]

Nuclear detonation would be the most devastating threat to commercial satellite capabilities.[43] The effects from a low-yield nuclear device, on the order of 50 kilotons, detonated a few hundred kilometers above the atmosphere would increase ambient radiation levels enough to severely damage nearby satellites and reduce the lifetime of LEO satellites from years to months or less.[44] Executing such an attack would require only a rocket and a simple nuclear device. Conventional ballistic missiles, when topped with pellet-laden warheads designed to fill a satellite's orbit with deadly debris, offer a third avenue of kinetic attack.[45]

Advances in miniaturization have enabled many countries to enter space with small, lightweight, inexpensive, and highly capable systems, and pose another means for attack. Microsatellites and nanosatellites, weighing 100 kilograms to 10 kilograms, respectively, are examples of such technology.[46] These products were developed to perform satellite inspections, imaging, and other functions but could be transformed into weapons. Placed on an interception course and programmed to home in on a satellite, the microsatellite could fly alongside a target satellite until commanded to disrupt and then disable it.[47]

If an aggressor lacked the ability to knock satellites down, he could simply choose to jam them. Jamming is the deliberate use of electromagnetic energy to disrupt an adversary's ability to receive electromagnetic signals and can be based on land, aircraft, spacecraft, or ships at sea.[48] Satellite communications can be disrupted by either radiating interfering power into the ground terminal's antenna or by directing interference at the satellite.

A final means of disabling satellites would be to attack associated satellite ground stations. Such specialized facilities are critical to the continued operation and effective use of a satellite and often are the most vulnerable to disruption.[49] Attack can be accomplished by a variety of means ranging from physical attack to computer network intrusion.[50]

The Implications of Satellite Vulnerability

Reliable and secure infrastructure is a foundation for creating wealth and improving national quality of life.[51] As vital functions of the government become increasingly reliant on Internet connectivity, the potential for catastrophic consequences exists if the ability to transmit data should become incapacitated. The conduits that relay critical information are susceptible to various means of attack. With the Internet becoming a primary avenue of communication, the potential disruption of vital chokepoints could wreak havoc on a nation. If an adversary were to attack a singular point that the bulk of communications from computer systems, people, organizations, and functional entities must pass through, paralysis could result. Functions as disparate as electronic-based funds transfers, travel-related services, communication between vital governmental organizations, and the operations of companies whose workforce operates away from a centralized location would be affected, which would potentially lead to catastrophic consequences.[52]

Denial of satellite capability might also affect global financial transactions. The impact would be primarily derived through stemming the fiscal capabilities of transnational corporations.[53] Worldwide outflows of foreign direct investment have increased at an annual average rate of 29 percent since 1983.[54] These investments are primarily attributed to the world's 60,000 transnational corporations and represent about a quarter of the world's economic input.[55] Limiting the communications capabilities of these companies would greatly reduce their capacity to operate normally and produce substantial disarray in global financial markets.

While primarily aimed at the civil and business sectors of a nation dependent on Internet access via satellite, these threats would also impact the defense sector. If commercial industries that provide key supplies or services to the defense department were to suffer, the attacks would undermine the nation's ability to provide logistical support, impeding the deployment and operation of defensive or expeditionary military forces in a variety of settings.[56] Furthermore, while it is acknowledged that much of the United States will ultimately utilize fiber optic solutions to resolve current bandwidth limitations, some remote U.S. bases and all U.S. ships at sea will remain dependant on satellites for a significant portion of their logistical support. Dependence on these technologies is exacerbated by the increased use of commercial assets within the defense department for this routine but essential routing of data.

Attacks on satellites used to relay Internet transmissions could also affect public opinion in key allied countries, introducing delays in coalition formation and coherence.[57] As noncooperative parties emerge, they could provide a haven for malefactors who could further aid in the compromise of infrastructure.[58]

As the world becomes more interconnected, the ability to effectively deal with international stress hinges upon the ability to communicate with foreign partners both economically and militarily. Unfortunately, the assurance of this capability seems to be in question, as the most likely avenue to growing global bandwidth will be vulnerable to myriad threats possessed by a wide array of nations.

Conclusion

As the economy becomes more globalized, economically competitive nations will need to seek the technologies that most efficiently provide worldwide connectivity. One of the lynchpins of this effort will be the Internet, which will emerge as a predominant form of communication in developing nations.[59] Because of a lack of existing telecommunications infrastructure, satellites will be an attractive tool with which to meet increased data transfer requirements, especially in developing countries where mature telecommunication infrastructure does not exist. However, because there are numerous technologies that offer the means to disrupt satellite communications, nations that become reliant on Internet communication via satellite may find their national infrastructure and business capacity at greater risk. While this vulnerability will directly affect nations that become reliant on Internet capabilities passed through satellite communications, it will also have indirect repercussions on the allies of such nations and the overall well being of the global financial structure. The international community needs to acknowledge these potential dangers and take action to develop a policy to resolve known deficiencies.

Notes

1. Donald Evans, "Remarks before the Global Internet Summit," March 7, 2001, Reston, VA, accessed April 25, 2001, http://www.inist.goc/speeches/evans_030701.htm.
2. Ibid.
3. This is a process by which applications are directly cached onto a hard disk and stored until the user desires. Smart technologies will conform applications to individual desires and traits.
4. Hans Binnedijk, ed., *Strategic Assessment1999—Priorities for a Turbulent World* (Washington, DC: Institute of National Strategic Studies—National Defense University, 1999), p. 38.
5. International Chamber of Commerce, "Note from the Secretary General to the G7 Countries," June 22, 1997, Denver, CO, accessed April 25, 2001, http://www.uscib.org/global/iccdenvr.htm.
6. Christopher Stix, "Bright Prospects Despite a Difficult Road Ahead," *US and the Americas Investment Perspective* (New York: Morgan Stanley Dean Whiter, 2000), p. 189.
7. William Perry, "Internet Becoming a Major Tool in Growth of International Trade," *Charleston Regional Business Journal,* 19 June 2000, accessed April 25, 2001, http://www.crbj.com/articles/2000/06192000/Internet. This article quotes numerous projections provided by Forrester, Inc, a leading Internet consulting company.
8. Ibid.
9. President's Commission on Critical Infrastructure Protection, *Critical Foundations—Protecting America's Infrastructures* (Washington, DC: Government Printing Office, 1997), p. 11.
10. Merrill Lynch, "Global Satellite Marketplace 2001," *US Telecommunications Perspective* (New York: Merrill Lynch, 2001), p. 4 (all rights reserved).
11. George Gilder, *Telecosm: How Infinite Bandwidth Will Revolutionize Our World* (New York: The Free Press, 2000), p. 9.
12. Craig Freudenrich, "How Fiber Optics Work," accessed April 28, 2001, http://www.howstuffworks.com/fiber-optic1.htm.
13. Mel Mandell, "120,000 Leagues Under the Sea," *Institute of Electronic and Electrical Engineers Spectrum* 37, no 4 (April 2000): p. 64.
14. Craig Freudenrich, "Question of the Day," accessed April 28, 2001, http://www.howstuffworks.com/question402.htm.
15. SBC Communications, "DSL vs Cable Modems," accessed April 28, 2001, http://www.pacbell.com/UDSL/content/1,5143,3,00.html.

16. Andy Reinhardt, "What Could Whip the World Wide Wait," *Business Week,* February 16, 1998, accessed March 22, 2001, http://www.businessweek.com/1998/07/b3565114.htm. For reference, current analog modems over cooper wires transmit at 56,000 bits per second.

17. Dudley Fishburn, ed., *The World in 2001* (London: The Economist Group, 2000), p. 94.

18. U.S. Department of Commerce International Trade Administration, *U.S. Industry and Trade Outlook 2000* (New York: McGraw Hill Companies, 2001), chapter 29, p. 14.

19. Ibid.

20. Linda Haller, "Commercial Space and United States National Security," in *Commission to Assess United States National Security Space Management and Organization—Report to Congress Pursuant to Public Law 106–65* (Washington, DC: Government Printing Office, 2001), 14. This work is an appendix to the report.

21. Ibid.

22. Ibid.

23. Vijay Jayant, "Metamorphosis," *US and the Americas Investment Perspective* (New York: Morgan Stanley Dean Whiter, 2000), p. 173 (all rights reserved).

24. Merrill Lynch, "Global Satellites," p. 3.

25. GSM World, *Thuraya Satellite Telecommunications Company,* accessed April 28, 2001, http:// www.gsmworld.com/technology/thuraya.html.

26. The area that a single satellite can service on the ground. AcES's coverage is 11 million square miles (including 80 percent of China); Thuraya's covers the Indian subcontinent, the Middle East, Central Asia, North and Central Africa, and Europe.

27. GSM World, *Thuraya.*

28. Office of Space Commercialization, *Trends in Space Commerce: Report for the Secretary of Commerce* (Washington, DC: Government Printing Office, 2001), chapter 3, accessed June 18, 2001, http://www.ta.doc.gov/space/library/reports. For additional information, see http://www.futron.com/pdf/2000YIR/PDF.

29. Office of Space Commercialization, *Trends in Space Commerce.*

30. Ibid.

31. Captain Ned Bagley, USN, Chief Of Naval Operations staff, Information Superiority Division, interview by author, April 23, 2001, Crystal City, VA.

32. Mandell, "120,000 Leagues," 64. Satellites in GEO have a .25 to .5 second delay in transmission.

33. Office of Space Commercialization, *Trends in Space Commerce.*

34. Ibid.

35. According to Nua Ltd., an Internet consulting firm, in June of 2000 there were 304 million people online, with over 700 million expected by 2005. Individual web pages will grow from 800 million to over 1 billion over that same period. Business-to-business and business-to-consumer e-commerce are expected to rise 300 percent and 125 percent respectively from 1998 to 2003. http:www.crbj.com/articles/2000/06192000/Internet.

36. Merrill Lynch "Global Satellite," p. 4.

37. Haller, "Commercial Space," p. 50–51.

38. Commission to Assess United States National Security Space Management and Organization, *Report to Congress Pursuant to Public Law 160–65* (Washington, DC: Government Printing Office, 2001), chapter 2, p. 17. Hereafter referred to as Rumsfeld Report.

39. Michael Callaham, *Anti-Satellite Weapons, Countermeasures and Arms Control* (Washington, DC: Office of Technology Assessment, 1985), p. 67–69.

40. James Lee, *Counterspace Operations for Information Dominance* (Maxwell AFB, AL: Air University Press, 1994), p. 31.

41. An EMP can be created by using a flux compression generator (developed in the late 1950s), and a high power microwave source. A technical diagram of this technology can be found at http://www.infowar.com/mil_c4/mil_c4i8.html-ssi.

42. Ibid., p. 3.

43. Rumsfeld Report, chapter 2, p. 21.

44. Ibid.

45. Joseph Nye, *Seeking Stability in Space: Anti-Satellite Weapons and the Evolving Space Regime* (Lanham, MD: University Press, 1987), p. 7.

46. Rumsfeld Report, chapter 2, p. 20.

47. Ibid.

48. Tim Bonds and others, *Employing Commercial Satellite Communications: Wideband Investment Options for the Department of Defense* (Santa Monica, CA: RAND, 2000), p. 71. Microwave weapons (such as those discussed in the EMP section) are designed to emit high-power microwaves for the purpose of causing permanent damage to receiving systems and are not included in this class of anti-satellite techniques.

49. Ibid.

50. Rumsfeld Report, chapter 2, p. 19.

51. Presidents Commission on Critical Infrastructure Protection, chapter 1, p. 3.

52. Willis Ware, *The Cyber-Posture of the National Information Infrastructure* (Santa Monica, CA: RAND, 1998), p. 29–30.

53. United Nations Conference on Trade and Development, *World Investment Report, 1999, Foreign Direct Investment and the Challenge of Development* (New York: United Nations, 1999), p. 2, accessed April 28, 2001, http://www.unctad.org/en/docs/wir99ore.pdf.

54. Ibid., p. 1.

55. Ibid., p. 3–8. Foreign affiliates had combined sales of about $11 trillion in 1998.

56. Richard Hundley, *Security in Cyberspace: Challenges for Society* (Santa Monica, CA: RAND, 1996), p. 17.

57. Ibid., p. 16.

58. Ibid., p. 33.

59. Eleven percent of the world's Internet service providers use a satellite link to connect to the Internet backbone. Jeff Morris, "B-to-B Satellite Internet Access Will Yield Near and Long Term Success," *Launchspace Magazine* (June 2000).

PART TWO

Information Technology, Freedom, and Civil Society— Case Studies

CHAPTER 6

Fujimori Meets Cabinas Publicas: The Internet, Journalism, and Democracy in Peru

Richard Hughes

The will of the people is the only legitimate foundation of any government, and to protect its free expression should be our first object.

—Thomas Jefferson

As for the opposition, what can it do? Engage in civil disobedience or non-violent protest until Fujimori resigns or agrees to a new, cleaner election? Montesinos' intelligence forces are anything but civilized."

—Robert T. Buckman, *Latin America 2000*

Peru has undergone numerous struggles over the last decade. Many of its challenges are similar to those experienced by other Latin American nations: social inequality, stagnant economic development, and armed insurgency. In 2000, Peru seemed to be headed for another common

Latin American malady—autocratic or military rule. Faced with increasing criticism of his regime, President Alberto Fujimori seemed poised to preempt Peru's democratic government. Yet, at this critical juncture, public outcry, mostly from within Peru itself, forced Fujimori into exile in Japan and restored democratic governance. During this tumultuous period, the Internet, although still at a nascent stage of development within Peru, played an intriguing role in allowing liberal democratic values to come to the forefront. The Peruvian experience suggests that, even when available only to small segments of the populace, information technology has the potential to make unexpected changes in a nation's political landscape.

Social Inequality and Terrorism

Peru, the largest of the so-called Andean countries, was at one time the cradle of one of the world's most advanced civilizations, the Inca Empire. Despite this proud past, social discord, rooted in 200 years of Spanish colonial domination, led to a devastating insurgency that almost ripped Peru apart from 1985 to 1995.

Like so many other postcolonial nations, Peru experienced its own leftist/radical movement. The Communist Party of Peru for the Shining Path of Jose Mariategui, or Sendero Luminoso (Shining Path), was born as a splinter of Peru's more orthodox communist parties. Its philosophy was grounded in the Marxist writings of Mariategui (1895–1929), generally considered the father of the Peruvian Left; he was a mestizo (of mixed Spanish and Indian heritage) who believed that a communist state could be built in the tradition of the Inca empire.[1] The Shining Path espoused a strongly antigovernment and anti-Western doctrine that condoned the use of violence to achieve control of the country.

The growth of the Shining Path was linked closely to government neglect of rural areas. As a general rule through the late 1980s, Peru's central government prioritized the provision of services (communication, transportation, water, sewage, etc.) to the nation's urban (mostly Spanish) population before serving rural (mostly indigenous) areas.[2] The lack of basic social equality for the Indian people, Peru's severe economic decline during the 1980s, and the nature of Peruvian democracy—including a corrupt justice system—further abetted the Shining Path's rise.[3]

Against this backdrop, the Shining Path began a new urban campaign of terrorism designed to destabilize Peru's democracy. Utilizing bombings, armed assaults, and assassinations, the Shining Path began to focus on foreign businesses as well as government targets within Lima and the surrounding area. In 1984, the Tupac Amaru Revolutionary Movement (MRTA), an urban-based terrorist group, joined the antigovernment battle. Named after an eighteenth-century Peruvian Indian who revolted against Spanish rule, this group specialized in bombing attacks. With two major terrorist groups threatening to topple Peru's fragile democracy, the only saving grace for the government's embattled security forces was that the Tupac Amarus and Senderistas sometimes attacked each other as well as the government.[4]

Enter Fujimori

When Alberto Fujimori took office in 1990, the situation was dire. Peru's economy was in shambles and the terrorist threat seemed insurmountable. One of the barriers to effective counterterrorism was Peru's ineffective court system. U.S. Congressional hearings in 1992 noted that "corruption in [Peru's] judiciary was leading to the release of narcotraffickers and, indeed, to Shining Path leaders."[5]

Fujimori's solutions were ambitious. Born in Lima to Japanese immigrant parents, Fujimori was endearingly called "el chino" [literally "the Chinese"] by those of Indian origin who felt that he, like them, stood outside the ruling elite, who were predominantly of European ethnicity. He announced one of the most ambitious programs of economic reform in Latin America[6] and laid out a "Comprehensive Strategy" that involved economic reform, a "hearts and minds" approach to rural insurgency and continued expansion of police and intelligence capabilities.[7] Fujimori explained his plan partly by contrasting it to earlier government tactics: "[T]he army is not entering to [sic] the rural community where terrorists is [sic] present with weapons and munitions. They are entering with a machinery for building roads, improving the irrigation system and taking benefits for the people."[8]

At the same time, Fujimori managed to establish a more cooperative relationship with the military and security agencies, focusing their efforts on antiterrorist activities.[9] He significantly enhanced the Military Intelligence Bureau, known as SIN, and coordinated their efforts with the antiterrorist police intelligence arm (more analogous to the U.S. Federal Bureau of Investigation). He also began a long-term association with Vladimir Montesinos, the shadowy head of the SIN, who coordinated much of his antiterrorist activity and was also the primary point of contact for U.S. CIA assistance.[10] Although the United States did not provide much financial aid, Washington's deep concern about the connection between terrorism and narcotics trafficking led to U.S. intelligence agency support of Peruvian security forces, including intelligence and training to help combat the Shining Path.

On April 5, 1992, Fujimori took his aggressive stance against the ongoing insurgencies a step further. In an *autogolpe* (self-coup) he unilaterally abrogated Peru's constitution and shut down the Peruvian Congress. This action allowed him to assert wide-ranging executive powers, including broad new definitions for terrorism and treason, and to institute a system of "faceless" civilian and military courts, in which prosecutors' and judges' identities were not revealed to protect them from terrorist intimidation.[11] Tactically, Fujimori's moves paid off: On September 12, 1992, the leader of the Shining Path, Abimael Guzman, was captured at a safe house in Lima, along with other members of the movement's leadership.

Guzman had been a cultlike figure, and his capture shook the organization. Deprived of leadership and popular support, the Shining Path became increasingly vulnerable to the efforts of Peruvian intelligence and police agents. Total terrorist actions in Peru fell from 2,995 in 1992 to 883 in 1996 and to only 310 in 1998.[12] Peruvian security forces turned the tide on the Shining Path during the mid-1990s, taking the initiative away from the terrorists and continuing to capture key leaders. In April 1995, police arrested 20 members of the Shining Path in the cities of Lima, Callao, Huancayo, and Arequipa, including a key leader, Margi Clavo Peralta, who later publicly announced her support for peace talks.[13]

The ultimate blow against terrorism was struck in response to the MRTA's occupation of the Japanese embassy in Lima on December 1996. The ensuing standoff was finally broken on April 22, 1997, when Peruvian commandos stormed the compound, killing all 14 Tupac Amaru members and losing only two commandos and one hostage.[14] The MRTA and Shining Path were both effectively broken, and significant terrorist activity in Peru subsided for the remainder of the 1990s.[15]

Authoritarian Government?

Although the terrorists were defeated, significant questions remained about the full restoration of Peru's democracy. Amnesty International repeatedly condemned Peru's judicial system for lack of due process in terrorist-related trials, excessive pretrial detentions, and the virtually unlimited powers granted to police when questioning suspects. Prisoners reported abuses by security forces including beatings, rape, electric shock treatments, and death threats.[16] Finally, the significant powers vested in SIN and other intelligence and security arms—especially the head of SIN, Vladimir Montesinos—became an increasing factor in Peruvian politics.[17] The security apparatus, previously directed at the threat of terrorism, became increasingly targeted at political opposition.

The success of the terrorist movement had convinced Fujimori, along with many supporters, that he was indispensable to Peru's continued security. Re-elected in 1995, Fujimori began to explore running for a third term as president. In 1997, when a constitutional tribunal declared this move illegal because Peru's constitution limited him to two terms, Fujimori's supporters in Congress dismissed three of the seven tribunal members.[18] Although the president's popularity—which had remained high during the suppression of the Shining Path's terror—plummeted, he remained firmly in control. If anything, his authoritarian actions, including domestic espionage, wiretapping, and harassment of political opponents and journalists, seemed to have "strengthened his grip on Peru."[19]

One example of Fujimori's heavy-handed tactics was the prosecution of Baruch Ivcher, the owner of Frecuencia Latina, a Lima television station often critical of Fujimori. In July 1997, when Ivcher broadcast several interviews critical of Montesinos and Peruvian security forces, Fujimori maneuvered to remove him as the station's owner. In 1998, after police issued arrest warrants for Ivcher and his wife, the persecuted station owner turned to the Organization of American States to plead his case. In July 1999, Fujimori reacted by withdrawing Peru from the OAS's Court of Human Rights and refusing to allow Ivcher to reenter the country.[20]

In 1999 and 2000, the crackdown on a free press continued. The Freedom House watchdog organization, in their annual report on worldwide journalistic freedom, downgraded Peru's status, from "partially free" press to that of "not free" press. The Committee to Protect Journalists listed President Fujimori as one of the "top ten enemies of freedom of the press" in both 1999 and 2000.[21] A U.S. State Department Report, issued in 1999, concluded that harassment of the media was an integral component in his effort to be elected for a third term as president."[22]

In April of 2000, a hotly contested election between Fujimori and Alejandro Toledo was fraught with allegations of wrongdoing, including intimidation of potential voters and ballot irregularities. In May, convinced that he would not get a fair contest, Toledo dropped out of a runoff election, guaranteeing Fujimori a third term as president. It appeared that Fujimori's strong-arm tactics had worked. Although the United States and others criticized the election, they were still willing to work with the president's regime.[23]

Crisis 2000

In September 2000, an obscure Peruvian cable television network, Canal N, broadcast a videotape of SIN intelligence chief Montesinos bribing a Peruvian congressman to support Fujimori, starting a precipitous crumble of the Peruvian strongman's regime.[24] At first, the president felt he could weather the storm, but as the ensuing scandal escalated, Montesinos was implicated in an arms-for-drugs deal with Columbian guerillas. In response, Fujimori fired Montesinos, who fled to escape prosecution, first to Panama and then, when Panama would no longer shelter him, back to Peru, where he apparently hoped to be sheltered by supporters. A countrywide manhunt for the former intelligence chief followed his return. Facing increasing public outcry, Fujimori agreed to hold new elections in which he would not be a candidate.[25] Tension built as opposition politicians feared a military coup, but eventually, on November 13, under increasing pressure from the Peruvian public and political opponents, Fujimori left the country, faxing his resignation from Japan.[26]

In the aftermath of his departure, civil society in Peru seems to have persevered. In April 2000, presidential elections were held, leading to a runoff contest between Alejandro Toledo and Alan Garcia, which Toledo won. United States president George W. Bush visited Peru in March of 2002, paying tribute to the progress of political institutions under Toledo's tenure.[27] Prosecutors are looking into allegations of corruption by both Montesinos and Fujimori, and recently Peru's highest court asked the government to seek Fujimori's extradition from Japan.[28] While Peruvian democracy still has many challenges ahead, the danger of a return to authoritarian rule seems to have passed.

Did the Internet Play a Role?

One important question about Fujimori's fall is why, unlike most autocrats, he did not simply shut down news organs to aid his quest to retain power. He appeared to have the backing of the military and much of rest of the apparatus of government, at least in the initial stages of the scandal. In part, this crackdown did not occur because of the government's inability to silence dissent before it could flourish. Dr. Catherine Conaghan, associate director of the Center for the Study of Democracy at Queen's University in Kingston, Ontario observed that, "The international monitoring of Peru, combined with insistent clamoring of the domestic opposition, made it impossible for the government to shut down the discussion of the regime's legitimacy and the need for democratic reforms."[29]

The rapid media development of the story was part of what made silencing dissent so difficult. Fujimori was inaugurated on July 28, 2000, the scandal broke in August, and he announced new elections in September and was out of office by mid-November; from a press perspective the flow of information was intense and received more international attention than most expected.[30] In such a rapidly moving situation, one potential contributor to the media's success in both broadcasting government misdeeds and igniting public indignation was its use of the Internet.

At first blush such a conclusion must surely seem dubious. Internet penetration in Peru is extremely limited; the most ambitious estimates show only about 400,000 Peruvian households are online, a mere 1.5 percent of the population.[31] The World Bank estimates that there were 3.09 Internet hosts per 10,000 Peruvians in 1999; in comparison Ireland had 156.68 per 10,000 the same year.[32]

This data is misleading, however. The nature of Internet access in Peru has been strongly shaped by one company, the Red Cientifica Peruana (RCP), a nonprofit consortium of Peruvian universities and nongovernmental organizations. RCP founder Jose Soriano adapted the concept of Internet cafes, using Peru's ubiquitous *cabinas publicas* (public booths). Users can rent access to the booths for prices ranging from $1.50 per hour to $15 per month. RCP, which hold upwards of 50 percent of Peru's Internet market, also provides free training on the use of the Internet.[33]

This unique mechanism for Internet access dovetailed nicely with the realities of Peruvian demographics. Lima, the capital city of Peru, holds much of the nation's population: Lima's 2000 population, by government estimates, was 7.5 million, almost 30 percent of the country's total population and almost ten times greater than the next most populous city, Arequipa.[34] Lima is at the very center of the nation's political life, and her citizens are much more likely to have access to information, from the Internet and otherwise.[35]

Interestingly, the Peruvian government, despite its numerous acts of censorship against print and broadcast media, actively encouraged Internet access. Although Fujimori may have been concerned, especially as dissent increased, about his critics' use of the web, he was much more interested in its economic value, and his government supported RCP's efforts to widen Peruvian's access to the web. During Fujimori's time in office, numerous government projects utilized the Internet, including an Internet-based, nationwide public registry (partially funded by the United Nations Development Program), a computerized archive of all Peruvian laws, and a statistical database of demographic information.[36]

Evidence indicates that, during the 2000 electoral crisis, the political opposition took full advantage of the government's lack of aggressive Internet censorship. A posting on the Democracies Online Newswire in April of 2000 contained a newsletter that organized anti-Fujimori activists for the upcoming election and included the URLs of web sites that provided polling locations, articles on previous election fraud and press freedom, and critical evaluations of Fujimori's second term in office. Links were also provided to all major election observers' web sites.[37]

A high percentage of Peruvian journalists have access to the Internet. A recently conducted study indicates that 91 percent of journalists in Latin America regularly use the Internet,[38] and the numbers in Peru are likely above that average. International journalists noted that increased access to the Internet in recent years has made filing stories from Peru significantly easier.[39] Although the number of Peruvians who receive information directly through the Internet may be relatively small, a much higher percentage may receive information that originated on the Internet indirectly through television or print media. The Internet also allows those journalists with access a much broader reach. As Marc Lifsher of the *Wall Street Journal*'s Andean bureau observes, "the Internet is now an essential tool for reporters gathering information quickly from a broad array of sources."[40]

Although it is possible to censor the Internet, it is done much less frequently and thoroughly than is the case with print or broadcast media. After all, what is to prevent citizens or journalists from accessing foreign websites that publish antigovernment information? Some governments such as Iraq or North Korea severely curtail their citizen's access to the web, others, such as China, utilize control of Internet service provider's (ISPs) to censor incoming content from abroad. Yet interestingly, the Peruvian government did not choose to employ either of these methods.[41] There is some evidence that Peruvian authorities attempted to limit the opposition's access to the Net by means of viruses that disrupted opposition newsgroups, but this did not appear to be effective.[42]

Conventional Wisdom or a New Paradigm?

Much of the coverage in the aftermath of President Fujimori's departure centered on the power struggle between him and his intelligence chief.[43] Other accounts detail the potential for a military coup and the role of international pressure in forcing Peru's strongman from power.[44] Yet what seems to be overlooked in these accounts is the powerful role that Peru's own press played in the demise of their president's regime. As Dr. Conhagan notes, "Independent print outlets (*La Republica, El Comercio,* and *Caretas)* and the broadcast media (Canal N and CPN Radio) made critical contributions in keeping the discussion of the legitimacy of the election and the regime on the front burner."[45] The videotape revelation of Montesinos' bribery, made by the tiny cable station Canal N (viewed by at most 100,000 households, all in Lima), was the impetus for Fujimori's fall.[46] Subsequent revelations in the written press were also instrumental, as newspapers rapidly spread the story to those without television access.

After the initial revelations, the normally media-savvy Fujimori seemed unable to control the erosion of public trust in his government. When he announced his departure he stated that the scandal had created a "lack of credibility" that forced his departure.[47] Also notable was the rapid reaction of the press corps at large. Not just opposition news agencies but virtually all journalists seemed to turn on the government. Even some previously progovernment stations began broadcasting damaging reports.[48]

Although the exact degree of impact cannot be measured, the increased volume of information disseminated via the Internet clearly played a role in the speed at which the Montesinos scandal hit the Peruvian government. Within days of Canal N releasing the videotape, stories appeared in major U.S., European, and Latin American newspapers and Internet news portals.[49] This made it much more difficult to contain or control the results. "The negative coverage of the elections and inauguration by the international media clearly demonstrated how completely Fujimori had lost the public relations war."[50]

While a previous government might simply have shut down Canal N, the Fujimori regime seems to have known that there were much broader mechanisms disseminating antigovernment information. Antigovernment protestors appeared to realize this as well. Student demonstrators used chants such as "Gracias pa su ayuda, la prensa extranjera!" (Foreign press, thanks for your help!)[51]

Another indication of the power of the Internet was found in the aftermath of the crisis as the Interior Ministry set up a website to aid in capturing Montesinos, the renegade intelligence chief, with "WANTED" plastered in red across the home page. Located at www.mininter.go.pe, the site urges anyone with information about Monetsinos's whereabouts to send e-mail to Peruvian authorities at www.captura+mininter. gob.pe.[52] This effort on the part of the new post-Fujimori government demonstrates its belief that the world wide web is accessed by key parts of the Peruvian population.

Conclusions

The scandals uncovered in the fall of 2000 that brought down the Fujimori government were not unique. The Peruvian strongman had faced similar challenges to his authority earlier in his tenure. What was unique was the rapid reaction of the Peruvian press to expose the corruption and galvanize public support against Fujimori and Montesinos. This synergy of an activist press, which was both Internet savvy and widely connected, both among themselves and internationally, seemed to catch the Fujimori regime flatfooted and unprepared for the magnitude of the public reaction that ensued.

The reasons why a democratic transition, rather than an authoritarian crackdown, resulted are certainly complex. Internal power struggles and international pressure were a part of the equation. But a powerful emergence of Peruvian liberal values, spearheaded by a newly activist press and enabled in part by the Internet and other information technologies, was also in evidence. This demonstrates that even in countries such as Peru, which has relatively low Internet penetration when measured against the total population, exposure of information technology to key populations can have important consequences.

Notes

1. Tarazona-Sevillano, Gabriela, *Sendero Luminoso and the Threat of Narcoterrorism* (New York: Praeger, 1990), p. 10.
2. Niksch, Larry A., *Peru's Shining Path* (Washington, DC: Congressional Research Service, 1993), p. 11.

3. Ibid., pp. 10–11.
4. Terrorism Research Center, *Profile of Tupac Amaru,* May 2001, www.terrorism.com.
5. Representative Robert G. Torticelli, U.S. Congress, House, Committee on Foreign Affairs Subcommittee on Western Hemisphere Affairs, *Situation in Peru and the Drug War,* 102nd Cong., 2nd sess., May 7, 1992.
6. Barbara Stallings and Wilson Peres, *Growth Employment and Equity: The Impact of the Economic Reforms in Latin America and the Caribbean* (Washington, DC: Brookings Institution Press, 2000), p. 205.
7. Alberto Fujimori, *Transcript of Speech to National Press Club,* September 18, 1991 (Washington, DC: Congressional Information Service, 1991).
8. Ibid.
9. Cynthia McClintock, *Revolutionary Movements in Latin America* (Washington, DC: United States Institute of Peace Press, 1998), p. 147.
10. Charles Lane, "Superman Meets Shining Path: Story of a CIA Success; With Agency Aid, Peru Captured Chief Rebel," *Washington Post,* 7 December 2000, www.washingtonpost.com.
11. Robin Kirk, *Peru: Two Faces of Justice* (New York: Human Rights Watch/ Americas, 1995), pp. 2–3.
12. Peruvian Government, Instituto de Estadistico y Infomatica, *Violencia Politica,* May 13, 2001, www.inei.gob.pe.
13. U.S. State Department, *Patterns of Global Terrorism 1995,* accessed May 13, 2001, www.state.gov/www/global/terrorism/gt_index.html.
14. Robert T. Buckman, *Latin America 2000* (Harpers Ferry, WV: Stryker-Post Publications, 2000), p. 227.
15. U.S. State Department, *Patterns of Global Terrorism 1999,* accessed May 13, 2001, www.state.gov/www/global/terrorism/gt_index.html.
16. Amnesty International, *Peru: Anti-terrorism Laws Continue to Fall Short of Human Rights Standards,* AMR 46/05/94 (Washington, DC: Amnesty International, 1994), p. 2.
17. Christopher Marquis, "U.S. Says Asylum in Panama Helped Avert a Coup in Peru," *New York Times,* 26 September 2000. See also Anthony Faiola, "Top Military Commanders Ousted by Peru's Fujimori," *Washington Post,* 29 October 2000.
18. Anthony Faiola, "Fujimori as Emperor: No Longer Just a Joke; Peruvian President's Popularity Plummets Amid Mounting Accusations of Abusing Power," *Washington Post,* 11 August 1997.
19. Ibid.
20. Buckman, *Latin America 2000,* pp. 227–228.
21. Catherine M. Conaghan, "Agenda Paper No. 47: Making and Unmaking Authoritarian Peru: Re-Election, Resistance and Regime Transition," The Dante B. Fascell North-South Institute (University of Miami: Lynne Rienner Publishers, Inc., May 2001), p. 7. Also available at http://www.miami.edu/nsc/pages/pub-ap-pdf/47AP.pdf.
22. U.S. Department of State, Bureau of Democracy, Human Rights and Labor, 2000, *Country Report on Human Rights Practices for 1999: Peru* (Washington, DC: U.S. Department of State, 1999).
23. Clifford Krauss, "Tensions Build for Inauguration in Peru," *New York Times,* 28 July 2000.
24. Sebastian Rotella, "After Fraud, Bribes, Videotapes, Peru Finds Hope in Disclosure," *Los Angeles Times,* 10 February 2001. See also Anthony Faiola, "In Peru, Candid Cameras Leave Audience Stunned; Fugitive Spy Chief Videos Expose Depth of Corruption," *Washington Post,* 4 March 2001.

25. Sebastian Rotella and Natalia Tarnawiecki, "Fujimori Has Peru Waiting, Wondering," *Los Angeles Times,* 18 September 2000. See also, Anthony Faiola, "Broad Praise for Colonel's Mutiny Underlines Peru's Instability," *Washington Post,* 31 October 2000.

26. Clifford Krauss, "Fujimori's Fall: A Nation's Lion to Broken Man," *New York Times,* 3 December 2000.

27. "Bush Backs Peru's War on Terrorism," *BBC News,* March 24, 2002, accessed June 9, 2002, http://news.bbc.co.uk/hi/english/world/americas/newsid_1890000/1890259.stm.

28. AP World Politics, "Peru Supreme Court Approves Extradition Request for Fujimori," May 30, 2002, accessed June 9, 2002, at *Yahoo! News,* http://story.news.yahoo.com/tmpl=story&u=/ap/20020531/ap_wo_en_po/peru_japan_fujimori.htm.

29. Conaghan, "Agenda Paper No. 47," p. 2.

30. Telephone interview with Lucien Chauvin, *Washington Post* staff writer, December 19, 2001.

31. Jupiter Communications 1999 estimate available at NUA Internet Surveys Web Site, May 5, 2001, www.nua.ie/surveys/how_many_online/s_america.html.

32. *World Bank Development Indicators, 2000* (New York: United Nations International Bank for Reconstruction and Development, 2000), p. 297.

33. Noah Elkin, "Internet Power to the People," *eMarketer,* March 8, 2001, accessed May 5, 2001, www.emarketer.com/analysis/elatin_america/20010308_internet_power.html.

34. Peruvian Government, *Instituto de Estadistico y Infomatica,* May 13, 2001, www.inei.gob.pe/inei4/percifra/inf-dem.

35. Government statistics indicate that while some 55 percent of residents in Lima and surrounding areas have a computer, a mere 5 to 8 percent of the rest of the nation do. This is also true of phone service: about 95 percent for Lima, less than 60 percent in the rest of the country. Peruvian Government, *Organismo Supervisor de Inversion Privada en Telecomunicaciones* (OSIPTEL), "Indications of Internet Access," May 5, 2001, www.osiptel.gob.pe.

36. These can be found at www.orlc.gob.pe, www.minjus.gob.pe, and www.inei.gob.pe, respectively. Georgia Scott, "Peru's Government Goes High Tech," *UN Development Program: Information and Communications Technology,* United Nations web site, May 13, 2001, www.sdnp.undp.org/it4dev/stories/peru.html.

37. Cesar Gayoso, "Boletin Electronico sobre Campanas Politicas," online posting, April 10 2000, *Democracies Online Newswire,* accessed May 5 2001, www.e-democracy.org/do (search for "Peru").

38. Daniel Helft, "Journalists Lead Latin America on the Web, Study Says," May 1, 2001, *The Standard,* accessed May 6, 2001, www.thestandard.com/article/0,1902,24122,00.html.

39. Telephone interview with Andrew C. Benson, *Washington Times* staff writer, December 20, 2001.

40. Telephone interview with Marc Lifsher, *Wall Street Journal,* Andean bureau, December 29, 2001.

41. Leonard R. Sussman, "Censor Dot Gov: The Internet and Press Freedom 2000," *Freedom House: Press Freedom Survey 2000,* accessed May 2, 2001, www.freedomhouse.org/pfs2000/sussman.html.

42. The report of a (presumably) government-spawned virus designed to disrupt the anti-Fujimori Libertad Desarrollo newsgroup (libertaddesarrollo@hotmail.com)

and the means to circumvent the tactic come via Cesar Gayoso, "More Peru—Cyber War by the Democracy in Peru," online posting, April 10, 2000, Democracies Online Newswire, accessed May 5, 2001, www.e-democracy.org/do (search for "Peru").

43. Krauss, "Fujimori's Fall."

44. Marquis, "U.S. Says Asylum in Panama Helped Avert a Coup in Peru."

45. Conhagan, "Agenda Paper No. 47," p. 28.

46. Interview with Lucien Chauvin.

47. Anthony Faiola, "Fujimori Calls New Elections, Will Not Run; Bribery Scandal Prompts Nationwide TV Address," *Washington Post,* 17 September 2000.

48. Matt Moffett, "Peru's Press Now Less Cowed by State—Bribery Scandal Emboldens Papers and TV to Report Much Less Reverently," *Wall Street Journal,* 28 September 2000.

49. These include several stories dated September 15, 2001, on the BBC website, radio, and TV coverage at http://news.bbc.co.uk/hi/english/world/monitoring/media_reports/newsid?926000/926915.stm, and one September 16 story in the *New York Times* Foreign Desk section, also published on the web (article archived at www.nyt.com), and several September 15 Internet and TV stories by CNN http://www6.cnn.com/2000/WORLD/americas/09/15/peru.scandal.sacrifice.reut/index.html. The BBC coverage indicated that all three major Lima daily newspapers, *La Republica, El Commercio,* and *El Expreso,* were "quick to condemn" the bribery scandal.

50. Conhagan, "Agenda Paper No. 47," p. 28.

51. Ibid., p. 29.

52. Reuters, "Peru Creates Web Site in Hunt for Former Spy Chief," *eMarketer,* December 27, 2000, accessed May 2, 2001, www.emarketer.com/estatnews/enews/12_27_2000.rwntz-story-bcnetperumontesinosdc.htm.

CHAPTER 7

Beyond the Internet: Democracy on the Phone?

Alessandra Cabras

For some years, the organization of free and fair elections was considered a sufficient condition for the termination of dictatorships and the establishment of democratic regimes. In 1993, elections were held in Burundi, where three successive military coups d'état had followed the country's independence in 1962. In Cambodia, after years of terror by Pol Pot and authoritarian rule supported by neighboring Vietnam, elections took place in 1993 as well. It turned out, however, that elections alone were not enough: Both countries experienced the return to power of former elite defeated by the electoral vote. The elections in the Philippines in 1986 and in South Africa in 1994 highlighted the importance of support for the democratic exercise by sound civil society, media, and a strong political opposition. Today's priority in the democratization process does not seem to be any longer the election as such; the crucial issues are stability, good governance, and empowerment of the populations.

Key in this context is the availability of information—to provide local populations and civil society organizations with greater leverage over national governments, and to allow different societies of the globalized world to interact in the most knowledgeable and suitable way. Today's technology, in particular the Internet, is instrumental in making available a huge amount of information and in breaking the chains of censorship most of all where freedom of the press is yet at its early stages.[1] In these and other ways, the Internet and e-mail could theoretically have a beneficial influence on the most basic human rights, in part by furnishing a valuable means of pressuring governments, groups, or individuals who violate them.

Governments responsible for human rights violations tend to control or even block the free flow of information. However, millions of bits of information already speed through phone lines, move across networks, and reach millions of people worldwide.[2] Satellite communication can help to bypass censorship and local telecommunications infrastructure.[3] This is true even in the areas of the world in development. For example, speakers at the Africa Internet Summit and Exhibitions (AFRINET), held in Abuja, Nigeria in October 2000, looked at the access to electronic information in the continent and agreed that liberalization and privatization of the African telecommunications industry is essential to increasing Internet penetration on the continent.[4]

The effect of information depends upon the nature of the country. In well-developed and democratic countries, radio, television, telephone, and, more recently, Internet and e-mail enable citizens to easily access information and communicate electronically—not only with each other but also with their elected representatives. In countries still in transition to full freedom, the Internet allows citizens and activists to avoid censorship if not retaliation. E-mail, much cheaper and faster than other communication systems, allows the exchange of information and electronic fora where national diasporas can be very involved and vocal. In addition, the Internet represents an important outreach instrument for nonstate actors, providing them with the ability to disseminate information worldwide. The web sites created by many nongovernmental organizations (NGOs), various institutions, numerous individuals, and some of the parties involved in or dealing with the conflict of the Great Lakes region in Central Africa exemplify this trend.[5] Nonetheless, the divide between developed and developing countries in this sector is important: In 1999 the number of Internet hosts per 10,000 people were 2.39 in East Asia and the Pacific; 15.47 in Europe and Central Asia; 14.78 in Latin America and the Caribbean; 0.37 in the Middle East and North Africa; 0.17 in South Asia; and 2.32 in Sub-Saharan Africa.[6]

The Internet has received the lion's share of the attention recently devoted to telecommunications technologies and their potential to affect politics. On closer examination, though, a different technology may already have had a larger impact on the democratization process worldwide[7]: mobile phones. Easier to carry and cheaper than computers,[8] mobile telephones played a role in Senegal during the 2000 presidential elections, ensuring a peaceful transfer of power, and in the Philippines in early 2001 in the organization of mass demonstrations aimed at ousting President Estrada. Mobile telephones have also been used in conflict situations: Individuals in the front armed with mobile phones can be even more important than those carrying guns. In particular, easier and continuous access to the international media provides technologically sophisticated groups and individuals with fame, authority, and leverage with their national and international audience. The experience of the Democratic Republic of Congo (DRC, formerly Zaire), since the march in 1996 to conquest Kinshasa that led to the ouster of President Mobutu, also reflects the impact of this surprising technology.[9] Mobile phones were important for political actors to reach out as well as for combatants in the battlefield.

According to the International Telecommunication Union (ITU), during the 1990s the rate of growth of mobile communication was fastest in the developing world: From under 5 percent in 1990, its share of global mobile communication rose to more than 20 percent in 1998.[10] The ITU ascribes this growth to several facts: (1) mobile networks can be installed more rapidly than fixed ones[11]; (2) prepaid cellular cards circumvent the need to qualify for a fixed or mobile postpaid service; and (3) users find the functionality of mobile telephone use extremely practical. According to the data provided by ITU, the world's mobile telephone subscribers rose from 90,641.8 (k) in 1995 to 318,892.9 (k) in 1998.

To assess the impact of the increasing use of mobile telephones,[12] I will examine recent developments in three countries—Senegal, the Philippines, and the DRC—with a focus on the role played by mobile telephones in democratization processes or conflict situations. Because they combine low-cost voice communications with possible access to the Internet, mobile telephones might be considered a more empowering tool than the Internet itself. On the other hand, in crisis situations and where manipulation of communications networks is a well-learned lesson and phone tapping easy to practice, the arbitrary use of mobile telephones might threaten human rights and jeopardize the democratization process.

Senegal

In August 1960, Senegal, independent from France and separated from Mali, became a republic with Léopold Sédar Senghor as its first president. By the mid-1960s Senegal had become a de facto one-party state. When Senghor retired in 1981, he was replaced by his prime minister, Abdou Diouf, who afterward won the 1983 presidential elections, and the following ones in 1988 and 1993. In 2000, for the first time in Senegal's post-independence history, two rounds of voting were required to elect the president. As the results emerged, President Abdou Diouf peacefully conceded defeat, and Abdoulaye Wade, who stood and lost in every presidential poll since 1978, became the new president of Senegal.[13] Mobile telephones played an important role in ensuring this very critical democratic transition.

In a very organized manner, journalists, in particular radio reporters, chronicled the election from polling stations all over the country. Thanks to their mobile telephones they were able to report immediately on incidents and to announce live on the radio the results of the counting of ballots as soon as the results were available, at first on the local level and then nationally. As a result, candidates, political parties, and partisans were forced to accept the outcome of the voting.[14] Timing was critical: It was the speed at which the results were announced that facilitated the peaceful transfer of power to the new president. Abdou Diouf conceded defeat very quickly; not only was fraud no longer an issue, but the election's rapid resolution helped to defuse the tension that had built up during the two voting rounds.[15]

Local journalistic and nonprofit leaders confirmed the importance of the cell phones. Bocar Niang, editor of Sud Quotidien, argued that mobile telephones were very important in preventing any rigging during the presidential election, and beyond that in facilitating beforehand the flow of information and interaction among Senegalese.[16] This pre-election preparation was critical: As Mr. Taoufik Ben Abdallah, project officer for the Dakar-based NGO Enda Tiers Monde, points out, if political parties, civil society, NGOs, and the media had not previously created an enabling environment for the journalists to be near the polling stations and ready to report, their mobile telephones would have been useless.[17]

The popularity of the new devices and the increased number of subscribers led to the privatization of the first mobile telephone provider company. Sonatel (Société nationale de télécommunication du Sénégal) was created in 1985 and privatized in 1997: The turnover reached 77.7 billion francs Communauté Financière Africaine (FCFA), the number of lines increased by 22 percent, and the number of mobile phone subscribers grew almost 300 percent. As a result, new competition, created by new providers established in Senegal, lowered the rates, increased the traffic of international outgoing calls, and increased the mobile subscribers from 6,000 in 1994 to 200,000 in 2000.[18] The freer flow of information helped to create an enabling environment so that the political transition could take place in a democratic and peaceful manner. In fact, the broader economic implications of the new industry in Senegal suggest that the telecommunications industry in developing nations can have an indirect enabling effect for democracy: It nourishes a new industry that creates new, well-paid jobs, thus underwriting the expansion of the middle class. On the other hand, in developing countries where telecommunication infrastructure remains in an embryonic stage or is in some way deficient, the supply response is not adequate and therefore the impact of the new technology is hindered.

The Philippines

The peaceful transfer of power within the political elite of the Philippines that began in 1946, when the country achieved its full independence from the United States, was interrupted in September 1972 by President Ferdinando Marcos. Citing the threat from "subversive forces," Marcos imposed martial law. After fourteen years of one-man rule, Marcos was defeated by Corazon Aquino in the 1986 elections—largely because of the activities of a strong and vocal internal opposition, "People Power"—and forced into exile by pressure from the United States. While failing in major reforms such as land reform, the Aquino presidency achieved a fundamental objective: the democratic transfer of presidential power at the end of the constitutional term. The latest presidential elections in the Philippines, in 1998, were won by the very popular vice-president and former film star, Joseph Estrada.[19]

On January 21, 2001, fighting a corruption scandal and a rancorous Senate impeachment trial, Estrada was forced to resign, and Vice President Gloria Macapagal-Arroyo was sworn in. "People Power II" had now successfully ousted the democratically elected president, who "allowed the economy to collapse and had, according to testimony in the Senate, engaged in systematic corruption."[20] And Joseph Estrada's fall from power was due in no small part to a simple but politically potent cell phone–based technology known as "text messaging."[21]

On January 20, 2001, 100,000 Filipinos responded to a broadly distributed wireless call asserting that the military would withdraw their support for Estrada if one million people massed at the shrine that commemorates the People Power uprising of 1986. "'No one knew where these messages originated,' said Narzalina Lim, a civil society leader and minister under former president Corazon Acquino, who replaced Marcos in 1986. 'They just appeared and within an hour or two tens of thousands of people had gathered. It was really "People Power" in action as there was no obvious leader to make the calls.'"[22] All the messages ended with the same three words: "pass this on."

Short message service (SMS) is the ability to send and receive text messages to and from mobile telephones.[23] SMS messages can be up to 160 characters in length; the cost of sending messages is less than that of making a call, and the capabilities of mobile phones have evolved to the point where they can both send and receive messages. This means that mobile handsets can be used not only to broadcast data services but also to compose and send messages. Beyond the evolving capabilities of mobile communication technology, the expansion of the Internet has put the means to send an SMS message into the hands of vastly more users: Web users can send messages into the wireless system, so that the number of potential users is not only increasing in proportion to the growth of mobile subscribers but in proportion to every PC connected to the Internet. Interestingly, the web site www.eLagda.com is in the process of collecting one million e-mail registrations and has sought contact information for mobile telephone subscribers in order to generate more anti-Estrada sentiments.[24] The web site indicates that text messaging has become a tool for information dissemination, news, jokes, or novelties associated with the political crisis.

It is, moreover, very difficult for an authoritarian government to use similar technologies to its advantage. According to Andrew Micu, an activist in People Power and observer of People Power II, the movement that opposed Estrada was so widespread and deeply rooted that any attempt to use the technology to manipulate the crowd in favor of Estrada would have been of no relevance.[25] The nature of the technology also affects the audience reached: More young people than old use mobile phones, and Micu stresses that the major difference between the 1986 and the 2000 movements was that in the latter a larger portion of protesters were youngsters. Mr. Michele Manca di Nissa, United Nations High Commissioner for Refugees (UNHCR) officer in Manila at the time of the events, stresses that People Power II is an example of true popular demonstrations and of people's empowerment.[26] Interestingly, too, the Philippine example demonstrated the potential for technology leapfrogging: All of this happened in a country where the telecommunications system was until very recently inadequate and unreliable. The number of main telephone lines per 1,000 people grew from 10 in 1990 to just 37 in 1996–98, and the number mobile subscribers per 1,000 people grew from 0 in 1990 to 22 in 1996–98.[27] Wireless phone lines can race past land-locked infrastructure and create an effective telecommunications network in relatively short order—a fact that cannot be good news to repressive governments.

The Democratic Republic of Congo

Following a roundtable conference with the main Congolese parties in Brussels, Congo became independent on June 30, 1960. At the end of 1965 Joseph Desire Mobutu took power, and in 1966 he created the party Mouvement Populaire de la Révolution (MPR). He was elected, unopposed, to three seven-year terms in 1970, 1977, and 1984, during which time he developed an intense personality cult. In 1990, pressured by the political change in eastern Europe and by increasing donor concern, Mr. Mobutu prepared a program to convert Zaire into a multiparty system, a program that included the organization of a constitutional conference, which ended in December 1992, to establish a transitional legislature, which never functioned. The beginning of the end started with the end of the cold war and of the support from the West. In 1996, two major events took place: It was made public that Mr. Mobutu suffered prostate cancer, and an armed rebellion against his regime began in Eastern Zaire.

Laurent Desire Kabila, a thirty-year-old declared opponent of the regime, surfaced as the leader of the rebel movement. Kinshasa fell on May 16, 1997, but in August 1998 a new rebellion in East Congo quickly erupted into a full-scale war involving the armed forces of six African countries (Zimbabwe, Namibia, Angola, Rwanda, Uganda, and the DRC). In July 1999, the heads of state of the six nations involved in the war signed a peace accord in Lusaka that even today remains to be fully implemented.[28] Upon the death of Laurent Desire Kabila in January 2001,[29] his son Joseph Kabila succeeded to the presidency.

No data about DRC's main telephone lines and mobile subscribers is available in the United Nations Development Program (UNDP) World Development Report 2000, nor in the World Bank 2000 world development indicators. The International Telecommunication Union (ITU) Development Report 1999 indicates that in DRC the number of mobile subscribers grew from 8.5(k) in 1995 to 8.9(k) in 1998—but more impressively, the latter number represents for the same year almost 30 percent of total telephone subscribers. Taking into account the well-known unreliability of the traditional telephone system, it is of no surprise that the use of mobile telephones surged as soon as 1993, with two domestic companies sharing the market. Too expensive for the average Congolese, the elite of the country benefit from and communicate with mobile telephones.[30] In addition, in light of the many areas of the country where mobile telephone companies are not able to provide service, satellite telephones come to the rescue.[31]

The relevance of mobile and satellite equipment in conflict situations emerges from the crisscrossing contacts among leaders, mediators, envoys, business people, and journalists, and thus from the importance of being able to reach out and of being reached.[32] The use of mobile and satellite telephones during conflict has become standard operating procedure for all new and old actors in the region. During the conflict, many leaders gave numerous interviews—leaders whose constituency, in several instances, was difficult to identify, whose popularity was difficult to evaluate, but whose impact was magnified by their access to telecommunications. In addition, according to some analysts, satellite telephones gave the anti-Kabila alliance the advantage of a high degree of tactical flexibility. Rebels confiscated and made use of radios and satellite telephones belonging to aid agencies based in Goma and shut down international mobile phone links to prevent any unwanted leaking of information.[33]

Telecommunications Technologies and Political Change: Some Conclusions

The impact of new technologies is twofold: They allow new forms of individual power and mass participation, and they underwrite new forms of privilege.[34] Compared to computers, mobile phones are cheaper, easier to carry, and easier to use. While the Internet has been getting all the press as the cutting edge of globalization, more people will be using wireless phones than surfing the Internet in certain key developing nations. Thanks to this new technology, both political discussions and political conflicts are increasingly played out simultaneously across the country and across the Internet by a global diaspora. The more accessible the technology, the wider is the opportunity for people to participate in a nonviolent confrontation.

Key again is the widespread access to information. A July 2000 meeting of the United Nations Economic and Social Council (ECOSOC) focused on "Information Technology in the Global Economy" and emphasized the increasing threat of marginalization posed by the growing digital divide between developed and developing countries.[35] Africa's connectivity divide offers the most extreme example: 98 percent of African Internet connectivity is at the extreme south and north of the continent, concentrated among its small, well-developed regions. According to Internet Domain Survey, in 1998 South Africa had 122,025 Internet hosts, Senegal 117, and DRC 4. An additional divide exists within each country between urban and rural areas. However, technological innovations and the falling costs of telecommunications are widening access and making global connectivity available to individuals and communities.[36]

An important question for the future centers on the one development that could dramatically undercut the effectiveness of wireless telephones as a social tool: technologies that allow repressive governments to listen in on the calls. A simple scanner is sufficient to listen to much wireless communication. On the other hand, second generation (2G) mobile telecommunication offers better quality and higher capacity at lower cost to consumers as well as improved security of voice and data transmission, because its digital signals are unintelligible to FM scanners and the bitstream can be easily encrypted.[37] Even in this case, however, since the export of encryption products to certain countries is not allowed, some versions of the Global System for Mobile Communications (GSM) protocol—used in Europe—is not encrypted and therefore not protected and easier to detect.[38] In the wake of the terrorist attacks of September 11, the U.S. government has rushed to pass laws easing restrictions on tapping wireless conversations—restrictions that do not, in any case, exist to begin with in undemocratic states.

The trend toward government surveillance of wireless communication was well underway even before September 11. According to sources from a "leak" in Germany in 1998, the European law

enforcement agencies were planning to create an international network of centers able to tap any form of telecommunications anywhere in Europe—be it data, encrypted or in clear form; mobile
telephony; the Iridium system; or other satellite mobile phone service
that may follow.[39] France alone has four powerful listening posts
around the planet that can intercept all the traffic handled by
international communications satellites. The U.S. "Echelon" program uses satellites developed and launched by the National Recon-
naissance Office to intercept calls handled by satellite and to tap
intercontinental undersea telephone cables and even local calls.[40] The
bottom line seems to be that there are no secrets for the big powers—
and very few for many others even with more modest interception
technologies.

It is also possible to control and restrict the flow of information
online via more traditional means. Censorship via proxy servers—
devices interposed between the end-user and the Internet in order to
filter and block specific content, taxation and telecommunications
policies that keep Internet accounts quite costly and thus beyond the
means of many,[41] and the countering of critical information with
overflowing supplies of progovernment information are all tactics that
are available to governments intent on dampening the liberating effects
of wireless technologies.

It is not clear if such tactics will continue to be effective. The global
telecommunication system is in a transition period to the telephone of
the third generation (3G),[42] which promises faster communications
services, including voice, fax, and Internet, the ending of global roam-
ing, and cheaper and easier communication by satellite. Under 3G,
mobile telephones will benefit from an interoperability of the terrestrial
cellular networks with satellite systems, enabling full global coverage.[43]
Traditionally, communication satellites have followed a geostationary
orbit—an orbit in which a satellite seems to stay over one point of the
earth. Because of the high altitude of satellites on that orbit, heavy and
strong equipment on the ground is required. Using satellites at lower
altitudes would avoid that problem. In this context, two low-earth orbit
satellite networks are already available: Iridium, designed especially for
telephony in areas that lack cellular coverage, and Orbcomm, which
offers better service for short messages like e-mail. Other emerging
networks include Teledesic and Sky Bridge, which unlike Iridium and
Orbcomm were designed especially for Internet use. The advantage for
the free flow of information is that any country that continues to block
all of these satellite systems may have a problem if its neighbors allow
the systems to be freely used.

According to some, by 2005 fewer than half of European mobile subscribers will use traditional second generation services. However, 2G will not fade completely but will continue to play a role in the region's less-developed mobile markets, most probably in countries where poor fixed-line infrastructure and services give mobile telephony an edge.[44] In this context, there is discussion about whether the digital divide will lessen within 20 years, or whether the technological divide within societies and between rich and poor nations will continue to worsen.

To those who are skeptical that the Internet can promote democracy,[45] the role of mobile telephones is unlikely to seem more profound. However, there is no doubt that information empowers citizens and that both Internet and mobile telephones are effective and rapid information providers. At one point the principal source of information in western countries was the newspaper; afterward radio and television took over. Today's immeasurable flow of information and speed in decision making in the global world calls for technology that helps foster widely inclusive discussions, with political ramifications—as has been evident in the cases of Senegal and the Philippines. The effect is not always benign—in the Congo, mobile phones almost surely helped the conflict to last—though their ability to become an effective tool in conflict prevention and resolution is undeniable.[46] When mobile phones allow wider access to information, rural areas included, it will be more difficult for coercive governments to rule without being held accountable for their actions. Mobile telephones cannot make democracy, but concrete past cases demonstrate at least this much: They can ease the transition.

Notes

1. Although direct censorship of Internet content has not been a significant problem so far in Africa, Sally Burnheim, the Freedom of Expression Institute (FXI), indicates that there is a trend among Sub-Saharan transitional democracies to use more subtle forms of censorship. She mentions among others methods the monopoly of existing telecommunications services and the complete control over the new technology in order to retain sole access to the revenue and exert a degree of control over users. Sally Burnheim, "The Right to Communicate: The Internet in Africa," *Southern Africa Media Law Briefing* 4, no. 3. (September 25, 2001), http://www.fxi.org.za/medialaw/communicate1.htm.
2. Because of the increasing volume of information and of networking, according to the Internet Society (ISOC), there has recently been a rise in the issues associated with governance of the global phenomenon of the Internet. For the Internet to reach

its fullest potential, it will need effective, practical, and reliable forms of self-governance. Don Heath, "ISOC in Internet Governance," *On The Internet*, January/February 1999, accessed September 25, 2001, http://www.isoc.org/oti/articles/0199/heath.html.

3. Michiel Hegener, "The Internet, Satellites and Human Rights," *On The Internet*, March/April 1999, accessed September 25, 2001, http://isoc.org/oti/articles/0399/heger.html.

4. AllAfrica, "Africa's Internet leaders call for rapid growth," October 4, 2000, accessed September 25, 2001, http://www.nua.ie/surveys/index.cgi?f=VS&art_id=905356083&rel=true.

5. Already a list of 22 websites can be easily found by entering a query into a search engine and using "DRC" as a key word, http://directory.google.com/Top/Regional/Africa/Congo,_Democratic_Republic_of_the/Society_and_Culture/Politics/.

6. World Bank, *2000 World Development Indicators* (New York: Oxford University Press, 2000), pp. 300–302.

7. Back in 1993, Cambodia was the first country in the world to identify the potential of mobile phones as substitutes to the fixed line telephone communication. As in Finland, in Cambodia there are more mobile telephone subscribers than fixed telephones. Asbel Lopez, "The South Goes Mobile," *UNESCO Courier*, July/August 2000, accessed September 25, 2001, http://www.unesco.org/courier/2000_07/uk/connex.htm.

8. In his message to mark World Telecommunication day, May 17, 2000, UN Secretary General Kofi Annan indicated that the theme of the day was mobile communications. He added "cheaper and quicker to install and easier to maintain than the traditional fixed-line networks, wireless communications offer developing countries new opportunities for enhanced access to basic telecommunications services. Such access is critical in a world where information and knowledge have become the very premise of progress." UN Press Release, "Secretary-General's message to mark the World Telecommunication Day—17 may 2000," SG/SM/7400, May 15, 2000, accessed on September 25, 2001, http://www0.un.org/News/Press/docs/2000/20000515.sgsm7400.doc.html.

9. James Rupert, "Warlord in Exile," *Washington Post Magazine* (September 17, 2000): W4. The article provides a colorful description of another example of portable telecommunication system impact. "General Mosquito," a rebel in Sierra Leone armed with a gun and a satellite telephone, "gained international fame" in the late 1990s.

10. International Telecommunication Union (ITU), "World Telecommunication Development Report 1999, Mobile Cellular" (Geneva: ITU, 1999), pp. 2–5.

11. As the ITU report highlights, in countries endangered by many land mines, like Cambodia and Mozambique, it is difficult to lay wires.

12. At the ECOSOC meeting of July 6, 2000, high level segment, President Alpha Oumar Konare of Mali said that there was a greater push for cellular phones in Africa than there was to erect local infrastructure. However, he indicated that he wanted to see each part of Mali linked through the Internet, so that reliable statistics and information could be made available, which would contribute to transparent elections and enhance communication within the country and among the populations. ECOSOC Press Release, "Control of Information, Communications, Condition for Modern Freedom President of Mali Tells Economic and Social Council," ECOSOC/5896, July 6, 2000, accessed September 25, 2001, http://www.un.org/News/Press/docs/2000/20000706.ecosoc5896.doc.html.

13. The Economist Intelligence Unit (EIU), "Country Profile Senegal," April 7, 2000, Washington, DC: Electric Library, Georgetown University Library, accessed April 2001, //db.eiu.com.

14. Brigitte Breuillac, "Abdoulaye Wade serait le vainqueur de l'élection présidentielle au Sénégal, " Le Monde, 21 March 2000. Doudou Sarr Niang, "Alternance An: Le jour où le Sénégal a basculé," Le Soleil, 20 March 2001. Discussing the role played by reporters during the elections, he defines the mobile telephone as a gadget that can prevent fraud.

15. Abou Abel, "A Tool for Transparency," The UNESCO Courier, July/August 2000, accessed September 25, 2001, www.unesco.org/courier/2000_07/uk/connex2.htm.

16. Meeting with Bocar Niang, Nairobi, April 2001.

17. Conversation with Taoufik Ben Adballah, September 2001.

18. "Le Modèle Sonatel," Jeune Afrique / L'intelligent (March 20–26, 2001): 58–59.

19. The Economist Intelligence Unit (EIU), "Country Profile Philippines," August 1, 2000, Washington, DC: Electric Library, Georgetown University Library, accessed April 2001, //db.eiu.com.

20. Seth Mydans, "People Power II Doesn't Give Filipinos the Same Glow," The New York Times, 5 February 2001, A10. The article reports different interesting reactions to the new popular action. Paulynn Sicam, editor of Cyber Dyaryo, said: "don't judge us by a standard version of democracy like you learn in the States. We are happy with our democracy." Alex Magno, a political scientist who was active in organizing political pressure against Estrada, stated: "Now, days after the event, all the constitutional imperfections are surfacing. We would have preferred a resignation, but things were moving very fast." Sheila Coronel, director of the Philippine Center for Investigative Journalism, indicated: "The alternative would have been anarchy, blood in the streets and a coup. Military factions were already plotting against him. His political enemies were aligning with labor unions and leftist organizations to plan strikes and demonstrations. And his loyalists were preparing to fight back."

21. "A Virtual Blizzard that Snarled Manila," The New York Times, 20 January 2001, A3.

22. John Aglionby, "Filipinos rally to oust the president," The Guardian, 20 January 2001, accessed September 25, 2001, http://www.guardian.co.uk/Archive/Article/0,4273,4120391,00.html.

23. OECD, "Mobile Phones, Pricing Structures and Trends," (Paris: OECD, 2000), pp. 66–72.

24. "Oust-Estrada Cyber-Campaign Goes on Second Gear," Business World (Manila, November 21, 2000): 10. In April 2001, the eLagda.com welcome message recited: "This started as an Erap-Resign movement, with the Internet as its primary medium of protest. Today, this site has been transformed into a vanguard site for good governance." An icon called "Text Brigades" opens a page where it is possible to join the network and receive text messaging. In light of the role played by text messaging during political crisis, elagda.com created text brigades to verify raw information before disseminating it to members of the network.

25. Conversation with Andrew Micu, Washington, DC, May 2001.

26. Conversation with Michele Manca di Nissa, September 2001.

27. UNDP Human Development Report, (New York: Oxford University Press, 2000), pp. 198–201.

28. The Economist Intelligence Unit (EIU), "Country Profile Democratic Republic of Congo," October 5, 2000, Washington, DC: Electric Library, Georgetown University Library, accessed April 2001, //db.eiu.com.

29. The Agence France Presse, January 17, 2001, reported that the news of the killing of Kabila reached the participants to the 21st Summit France-Afrique, January 18–19, 2001, Yaounde, Cameroon, at about midnight: "Seules sonnaient les telephone portables dans les halls de l'hotel."

30. Raymond W. Copson, "Zaire," CRS Issue Report, Foreign Affairs and National Defense Division, updated December 18, 1996, accessed September 30, 2001, http://www.fas.org/man/crs/96–037.htm.

31. Hrvoje Hranjski, "Ugandans, Congolese Rebels Clash," Associated Press, 7 August 2001, accessed September 30, 2001, http://www.undp.org/missions/drcongo/rcdnews31.htm. "Kabila shouts down Museveni," The Monitor, Kampala, 2 June 1999. Recounting his role in the crisis of the Great Lakes, President Yoweri Museveni of Uganda states that he contacted Laurent Desire Kabila by satellite telephone. Bruce W. Nelan, "Zaire's new order," Time 149, no. 19 (May 12, 1997), accessed on September 30, 2001, http://www.time.com/time/magazine/1997/dom/970512/world.zaires_new_or.html. Nelan reports that "Kabila refers to Museveni as a 'good friend' and speaks to him by satellite telephone at least twice a week."

32. Tido Mhando, "Kabila's last interview," BBC News, 23 January 2001, accessed September 30, 2001, http://news.bbc.co.uk/hi/english/world/africa/newsid_1132000/1132591.stm. According to his own reporting, Tido Mhando, invited to Kinshasa to interview Kabila, upon arrival dialed Kabila's mobile number and the president himself answered the phone. After the interview, Mhando recounts, the night before leaving Kinshasa, his telephone rang and it was Kabila himself, who wanted to continue the interview.

33. Reuters Limited, "Cybersurfing from a war zone," Daily Mail & Guardian, Johannesburg, 29 January 1999, accessed September 30, 2001, http://www.mg.co.za/news/99jan2/29jan-congo_internet.html. Howard Barrell, "Rebels slowly gaining on Kabila," Weekly Mail & Guardian, Johannesburg, 13 November 1998, accessed September 30, 2001, http://www.sn.apc.org/wmail/issues/981113/OTHER46.html. The latter article indicates that the rebels use U.S.-made Iridium satellite telephones that have world coverage. Barrell reports that according to analysts the seizure of the town of Kindu and subsequent successes were due to the innovative tactics related to the use of satellite telephones. Alan Little, "What goes around comes around," online posting, The University of Edinburgh, September 30, 2001, http://www.cpa.ed.ca.uk/edit1/15/goesaround.html. Recounting the fall of Kinshasa in May 1997, Little indicates that the town was saved by the army chief of staff, who signaled to the men of Kabila that he was prepared to make a deal. He also reports rumors that state that since the rebels got within mobile telephone range, there were contacts between the two sides.

34. Martin Hall, "Africa Connected," First Monday, 30 September 2001, http://www.firstmonday.dk/issues/issue3_11/hall/index.html.

35. ECOSOC Press Release, "Control of Information, Communications, Condition for Modern Freedom President of Mali Tells Economic and Social Council," ECOSOC/5896, 6 July 2000, accessed September 25, 2001, http://www.un.org/News/Press/docs/2000/20000706.ecosoc5896.doc.html. ECOSOC/5896 also reports on the contribution of the Economic and Social Commission for Asia and the Pacific (E/2000/73) outlining the recommendations adopted by the Regional Round Table on Information Technology and Development.

36. To circumvent poor infrastructure and to facilitate poor communities' access to technology, phone shops have been used in many countries. Phone shops consists of a number of telephone booths built into a freight container and connected to a cellular network via a digital telephone interface. Phone shops can be transported to any location where there is cellular reception and avoid the expense and delay of fixed line installations

37. International Telecommunication Union, World Telecommunication Development Report, 1999, Mobile Cellular (Geneva: ITU, 1999), pp. 15–16.

38. Sara Robinson, "Cell Phone Flaw Opens Security Hole," *Interactive Week,* September 17, 2000, accessed September 30, 2001, http://zdnet.com.com/2100–11-502889.html?legacy=zdnn.

39. Duncan Campbell, "Revealed: Secret Plan to Tap All Mobile Phones," originally published in *Observer,* 6 December 1998, accessed September 25, 2001, http://www.gn.apc.org/duncan/enfopol%5F98%5Fobs.htm. "Das Original Dokument, 1: ENFOPOL98, vom 3. September 1998," http://www.heise.de/tp/deutsch/special/enfo/6326/1.html.

40. Joseph Fitchett, "Spying from Space, US to Sharpen the Focus," *International Herald Tribune,* 10 April 2001, accessed September 30, 2001, http://www.iht.com/articles/16360.html.

41. Human Rights Watch, "The Internet in the Mideast and North Africa: Free Expression and Censorship," June 1999, accessed September 30, 2001, http://www.igc.org/hrw/advocacy/internet/mena/summary.htm

42. Catherina Maussion, "Les portables à prix casquant," *Libération,* 8 May 2001, Economie Section, N. 6213, p. 18. She indicates that taking into account the huge investment for the 3G launch, some providers are raising the price of today's services.

43. International Telecommunication Union, World Telecommunication Development Report, 1999, Mobile Cellular (Geneva: ITU, 1999), pp. 19–35.

44. Agence France Press, 30 November 2000.

45. John A. Daly, "Will the Internet Promote Democracy?" *Information Impacts,* September 2000, accessed September 30, 2001, http://www.cisp.org/imp/september_2000/daly/09_00daly.htm.

46. Ahmedou Ould-Abdallah, "Burundi on the Brink 1993–95, A UN Special Envoy Reflects on Preventive Diplomacy," (Washington, DC: USIP, 2000), p. 146. He indicates that a number of people described him as "alone in a country that he has been sent to pacify without troops, and whose weapons of appeasement are meetings, cocktail parties, T-shirts, mobile telephones, wheelbarrows, and seeds to give to political leaders and farmers."

CHAPTER 8

China, Democracy, and the Internet

Robert Peters

Two hundred and twenty-five years ago, Thomas Jefferson wrote, "when a long train of abuses and usurpations, pursuing invariably the same object evinces a design to reduce [the people] under absolute despotism, it is their right, it is their duty, to throw off such government and to provide new guards for their future security." These words, taken from the Declaration of Independence, inspired an entire generation of citizens to choose the path of revolution in order to overthrow an oppressive governing system. Today, it seems that thanks to modern, instant telecommunications technologies, the hope of freedom that inspired a great nation to be born may be spread to other parts of the world that still live under despotism. Thanks to the Internet, Chinese citizens, living in one of the last communist dictatorships in the world, are able to download and read that same declaration.

History teaches, though, that expecting a linear relationship between a new technology and freedom may be naive. Dictatorial governments have been very adept at learning to utilize new technologies in order to solidify their control. One of the most interesting questions for political science today looks for a verdict on the role of the Internet: Will it serve as a vehicle for the spread of liberalizing values and ideals, specifically democracy, or will it merely be subverted in a concerted effort by dictators as a means by which to better monitor public sentiment, root out discontents, and post progovernment propaganda in chat rooms and forums for the purposes of strengthening their own regimes? I will be attempting to shed some light on this question, and provide some possible answers, with a look at the most important case study of the Internet's effect in the world—the People's Republic of China.

Bates Gill, a China specialist at the Brookings Institution, puts it this way. "The information revolution presents an age old problem for a country such as China. On the one hand, taking advantage of new and important technologies, while on the other shielding the country from perceived 'polluting' or transforming effects."[1] This is an important conundrum because whether China will be a democracy or another totalitarian superpower will have enormous ramifications for politics, economics, values and strategic postures in the twenty-first century. Indeed, "there is no more important question than whether Greater China might some day become a democracy."[2] It would be hopeful to believe that the Internet could become a major force for progressive change in China, but a close reading of the real evidence—as opposed to the florid hopes of technology advocates—provides little reason to expect such an outcome.

Indonesia and the Dream of the Interconnected Revolution

In the late 1990s, the corrupt ruling regime of Indonesia, which seemed to operate for the express purposes of siphoning wealth out of the state and the Indonesian economy in order to fill the pockets of the Suharto and Habibie families, fell to a coalition of students, activists, and liberals. These protesters used modern telecommunication technologies in order to coordinate demonstrations and share and spread information among the populace and the outside world. Organizers used cell phones in order to create mobile command centers for protesters, fax machines to send data about the archipelago, e-mail accounts in order to retain anonymity, and, for the first time in a revolution, the Internet to gather and disseminate information about the holdings and deeds of the ruling families.

Reviewing these developments, commentators pointed to the Internet as playing a meaningful role in the revolution in Indonesia. "There seems to be no controlling the medium," one wrote, "which has thwarted people who had succeeded in repressing all sorts of free expression for more than three decades . . . [Activists] may be on the run from authorities, but are free to convey their propaganda on the web."[3] That same commentator went on to contend that:

> There is as yet no match for the speed and capacity of the Internet to disseminate information and views, making it a medium that is greatly superior to all others for that purpose . . . Internet cafes provide a printer for hire, users are able to obtain hard copies of the materials with a speed that is hard to estimate. Printouts of alternative news are then distributed down to the grass roots.

Indonesian students studying abroad were able to send information about the regime that was not available in Indonesia back to friends and colleagues at home. "It did not take [students] long to realize that cyberspace also afforded them the opportunity to talk about topics considered taboo back home, such as human rights abuses and the repressive policies of the Indonesian government."[4] As the populace realized the magnitude of corruptness, the ruling regime eventually collapsed and was forced to allow a democratic election to be held.

For many, it would seem that the Indonesian revolution, with its heavy emphasis on new technologies such as cell phones and the Internet, would be the first of many such upheavals throughout the developing the world. It was believed that with a large enough amount of people on the Internet, being exposed to the ideals of liberalism and democracy and all the benefits that they bring to the wealthy, free, developed West, widespread revolution and dramatic political transformation would be virtually inevitable. As such, many pundits and scholars publicly stated that it was only a matter of time before the Information Age, once it finally spread to all parts of the globe, would spur yet another wave of democratization.

Even before the downfall of the Suharto regime occurred, such ideas had become commonplace among the technology-savvy in the United States. As early as 1997, Walter Wriston wrote in *Foreign Affairs*: "information technology has demolished time and distance. Instead of validating Orwell's vision of Big Brother watching the citizen, the third revolution (telecommunications) enables the citizen to watch Big Brother. And so the virus of freedom, for which there is no antidote, is spread by electronic networks to the four-corners of the earth."[5] Wriston goes on to parallel information and value sharing in a village with information sharing on the Internet:

Small villages are known as efficient marketplaces of ideas. A village
quickly shares news of any innovation, and if anyone gets a raise or new
privileges, everyone similarly situated will soon be pressing for the
same . . . A global village will have global customs. Denying people
human rights or democratic freedoms no longer means denying them an
abstraction they have never experienced, but violating the established
customs of the village.[6]

In this view, the Internet is a leveler, where a person in Shanghai is able
to see the freedoms that are enjoyed in San Jose, California and
consequently demand that he too has the right and ability to choose
who is on his son's school board, what tax rates should be, and whether
or not to allow children of illegal immigrants to attend public schools.
This model envisions basic human desires, including jealousy, as bringing about profound social change.

Even Rupert Murdoch, not one known for liberal ideas or trendy
views, has contended that "advances in the technology of telecommunications have proved an unambiguous threat to totalitarian regimes
everywhere."[7] One observer states that:

Both the volume and form of communication made possible by electronic
technology are seen to greatly compromise, if not totally undermine, the
capacities of authoritarian regimes to blunt the circulation of opposing
views. Seizing printing presses and jamming broadcasting frequencies,
for example, is now a limited defense by authoritarian regimes against the
flow of information.[8]

If these sorts of sentiments are correct, then it is axiomatic that, as the
Chinese Communist Party (CCP) embarks upon a long-range intention
of getting hundreds of millions of its citizens online in order to harness
the enormous economic benefit of the Internet, it is sowing the seeds of
its own destruction.

The Promise of the Internet in China

The idea behind an Internet-spurred revolution in developing states,
especially China, has become so prevalent that a whole cottage industry
has sprung up with regard to the prospect. Nicholas Lardy, Senior
Fellow of Foreign Policy Studies at the Brookings Institution, believes
that Chinese president Jiang Zemin has doubts about his regime's
ability to stay on top of the tide of information flooding into and out of

China. Lardy says that "the [Chinese] government is going to be way behind the curve if they're trying to control the Internet," pointing out that the banned meditation group Falun Gong has used the Internet to communicate with others both inside of China and throughout the international community. "Have they succeeded in limiting the ability of such groups to organize? . . . I don't think so. They're still terrified."[9] Indeed, with an organization like the Falun Gong, which has a membership upwards of 100 million followers, roughly 60 percent of whom oppose the CCP,[10] it is understandable that Beijing would fear such a group, which could be able to effectively organize a concerted movement aimed at the overthrow of the communist regime via the Internet.

As Beijing continues down the road of liberalization that Deng Xiaoping began in order to enhance the country's economic clout, in service of its larger goal of superpower status, the Internet is being more and more used as a tool to spur commercial activity and business transactions. That the CCP would simply "pull the plug" on the Internet in China if organized protest grew to be a serious threat is doubtful. In a recent *Foreign Affairs* article, reprinted in China Online, a site popular with Chinese living both abroad and within the PRC, Nina Hachigian contends that as China's "exposure to the global economy grows, soon to be accelerated by membership in the WTO, Chinese businesses must embrace new technologies simply to stay competitive."[11] She goes on to point out that "today, anyone in Beijing can anonymously buy a prepaid Internet card and log in, surf anonymously at an Internet cafe, and use hard to trace, web-based email under an assumed name." One can even access the controversial Tiananmen Papers online in China as well as Taiwanese President Chen Shui-ba's conciliatory inaugural speech. "To a large degree, the Chinese government cannot direct how surfers use the Internet. Although self-censorship is largely effective for mainland sites, the government cannot stop someone determined to explore cyberspace beyond China's borders."

Hachigian seems to agree with the proponents of Internet revolution who contend that the Internet allows for liberal dissident groups to anonymously gather online in order to swap information, stories, and ideas about reform in the same manner that Indonesian students did prior to the fall of Suharto.

Hostility toward the government collects and builds in public cyberspace as it cannot in physical China . . . Criticism of China's environmental policy and of corrupt officials also appears regularly in the chat room of the official *People's Daily* and on university bulletin boards on line. On line conversations can be very politically charged, most likely because censors are overwhelmed and unable to delete sensitive content quickly enough.[12]

It is entirely feasible then that an Internet culture built upon criticizing the status quo could well spread to include more and more criticisms of a greater number of subjects as the number of Internet users increases.

As the criticisms increase both in number and in scope, it is not inconceivable that Chinese citizens would come to the realization that centralized communist authoritarianism is simply inadequate and unable to effectively deal with the problems facing the PRC. As such, another political system that would be viewed as being more competent in dealing with such problems would be demanded, thus paving the way for a popular, Internet-driven political revolution resulting in either another form of authoritarianism or quite possibly, democracy. As long as either form of governance seems to have more potential effectiveness at dealing with imminent domestic concerns, *and* the CCP looks vulnerable of being ousted, a substantial political transformation could occur within the PRC. Such a transformation would more likely take on a democratic rather authoritarian form, due to the nature of the increasing complaints voiced by *individuals* via the Internet about the communist governing system. The reason for this is that these individuals who brought about the downfall of the communist system would most likely choose to retain their newfound political power, as it is inherent in people to retain (if not accumulate) as much personal power as possible.

As such, it would seem that a democratic transformation is not only possible but probable once Internet usage in China reaches a certain portion of the population. Usage of the web continues to skyrocket in China. As of the spring of 2001 there were 22.5 million Internet surfers in China, with the number expected to increase to at least 33 million by 2003 and 85 million by 2005.[13] Should these numbers continue to grow at a constant rate, the number of users dedicated to democracy would likewise grow (so the theory goes), thus weakening the hold of the communist party and bringing about more liberal values, if not a full transition to an electoral political system. Indeed, studies have come up with a direct correlation between the amount of civil rights and liberties in a state and the rate of introduction of the Internet.[14] Many see a symbiotic relationship between the Internet and liberal values, viewing them as mutually reinforcing entities that feed off one another. If such a scenario is correct, then a communist party bringing the Internet to its people would be engaging in an almost suicidal gesture if the regime plans to retain power.

The CCP's Attempt to Regulate the Internet

But of course it would be naive to think that the Chinese leadership is ignorant of the power of the Internet or is doing nothing in an attempt to stifle the effectiveness of online democratization efforts.

The Chinese government has, for example, created ambiguous laws with the goal of squelching the free flow of information. It uses broad regulatory phrases that make it illegal for anyone to post "state secrets" or "spread harmful information" on the Internet in order to have plenty of judicial room to maneuver when deciding how and when to prosecute dissenters. It is also illegal in China to use the web for the "spreading of rumors, slander or other information via the Internet for the purpose of overthrowing the state government, overthrowing the socialist system, or breaking up the country, or destroying the country's security."[15] The vagueness of these laws provides Chinese security services with enormous latitude in selectively enforcing them, leaving open the possibility in the minds of China's netizens about being arrested. The result is a combination of self-regulation and state-enforced information control.

Internet service providers (ISPs) are also held responsible for any postings in sponsored chat rooms critical of the regime. ISPs are also hindered by an almost Orwellian set of press restrictions; the Chinese Propaganda Department has outlawed the use of "cyber reporters" and requires that all news be taken from official sites. This assurance of reporting news only from official sites is important, for the Chinese communist view of news is not necessarily based upon the dissemination of facts but of "truth," an important distinction. A Beijing textbook in "news theory" states that:

> The socialist news profession has even higher demands of the reality of news. It does not only demand that every situation, every fact . . . reflects objectivity in a manner that is accurate to reality, but it also demands that in relation to the totality of facts, it must provide for people objective realistic views to be helpful to people to penetrate these views of objective life and recognize the basic nature of society and its era.[16]

Consequently, ISPs and "independent" news sites in China all draw from the same source, one that is dedicated to the promotion of socialist ideals. As a result, the thousands of "Internet police" that PRC employs, who spend their days surfing the net looking for illegal or "dangerous" subject matter, are able to quickly and easily track down sites that use alternative forms of news information that deviate from the party line. As a result, "the possibility of being shut down by the government has encouraged self-censorship by Internet companies—which in turn has dampened online political communication."[17]

The PRC also bans many foreign sites from being accessed in China. Many of them are Western-based media outlets, including the *Los Angeles Times,* CNN, the *Washington Post,* the *New York Times, Voice of America,* and the *Wall Street Journal.* Along with these publications, the sites for the Taiwan government and Amnesty International are also off limits.[18] Moreover, the content of "foreign propaganda" released by news organizations on the Internet must all go through the Communist Party Central Committee's Foreign Propaganda Office, which acts as a further control on foreign news sources.[19]

China has also made using the Internet cost prohibitive to all except those they want to be on the Internet, namely young, urban male professionals who have college degrees and come from wealthy cities and the rapidly developing coastal special economic zones. In contrast to laid-off industrial workers or poor peasant farmers, this particular group of people has benefited from the economic reforms of the past twenty years, arguably making them a less likely source of rebellion, whatever their political views may be.[20] The income of the average Chinese Internet user is $4,185 a year, roughly four times the salary of the average Chinese urban dweller.[21] The average cost of Internet use is $10-$45 a month, with an additional $.25-$1.00 per hour fee rate.[22] Meanwhile, the cost of actually purchasing a computer is virtually exclusionary in China, thus lowering the spread of the technology to upper-class professionals and further lowering the availability of the Internet to potential revolutionary demographics.

Roughly one-fifth of all those who access the Internet in China do so through Internet cafes.[23] These cafes, for people who can't afford full-time access to the Internet on their own, or those who simply desire to surf the web anonymously, are increasingly coming under government scrutiny. Internet cafes and similar businesses that offer access to the web are required to register and obtain the approval of several governmental departments and go through regular recertification processes. The cafes are required to ensure that "subversive materials" are kept off the terminals while customers use them, and cafe owners are held responsible for any illegal activity that may occur from terminals within the store.

If the cafes fail to adhere to such regulations, they are subject to being shut down by any one of the provincial, regional, or municipal telecom administrations and by any public security, cultural, industrial, or commercial governmental departments that may deem content inappropriate or illegal. Indeed, Internet cafe operators may be found personally responsible and jailed if the offenses are found to be grave enough.[24] In the fall of 2000, a government crackdown of Internet cafes in the city of Fuoshon found most cafes in violation of law and responded by shutting down all cafes in the city, forcing any that desired to stay open to reapply for permits.[25] One business in Fuoshon was fined over $600 because an employee used profanity while in a chat room that he accessed from work.[26] Beijing also puts a 10 to 20 percent tax on Internet usage in cafes, further limiting the use of anonymous terminals.[27]

The result of all of these efforts by the Chinese government has been an Internet culture that is antithetical to the commonly held view of the Internet in the West. There is no ideological free-for-all on the Internet, but a dialogue characterized by self-censorship and government intrusion. Political dissension on the Chinese web is, by all accounts, quite low. Hong Kong, a city that still retains a great deal of political and cultural autonomy, has been a center for political dissidence in the PRC. Even so, says Eric Sautede, editor of *China Perspectives,* a Hong Kong–based academic journal, "I have always been amazed by the crazy hype about how the Internet sweeps in democracy. In China, the Internet is now more a tool of control than a tool of freedom."[28]

In fact, self-censorship has become so effective that Sohu.com, a popular Chinese web site, whose list of owners includes Dow Jones & Co., warns users that the company that owns the site is "legally bound to report any Chinese citizens who post statements critical of the Chinese government."[29] King Lai, CEO of Netease.com, one of China's leading Internet portals, had the following to say about self-censorship while attending the 2001 World Economic Forum's China Business Summit: "Regulation in China is not about the Internet, but about content, regardless of whether it is TV, radio, newspaper or Internet. You don't go against the state, don't reveal state secrets, don't go against the 'one China principle,' no profanity that might destabilize the country, such as Tiananmen Square or the Falun Gong."[30]

When self-censorship fails, however, authorities do step in and make public arrests, in order to deter others from pursuing similar courses of actions. On June 3, 2000, Huang Qi and his wife Zeng Li were arrested for operating the antigovernment site "6–4Tianwang.com," which provided information on missing people, human rights abuses, and corruption within the PRC. They were formally charged with subversion for reporting on the May 30 trial of Qi Yanchen, a journalist who covered social instabilities in China and was sentenced to 15 years imprisonment after a trial that lasted for half a day.[31] Jiang Shihua, who frequently posted antiregime sayings on public Internet forums, was imprisoned for anonymously posting the sentence "overthrow the communist party." Due to these and many similar stories, China has become the "world's leader in jailing journalists," according to the Hong Kong–based Voice of Democracy, an Internet-based site devoted to democratic reform in China.[32]

Meanwhile, the CCP has been very effective at using the Internet to counteract antiregime sites. While the Falun Gong is able to disseminate their teachings via the Internet and was able to organize a 10,000 person sit-in in front of the communist leadership compound in Beijing two years ago, the CCP responded by simply shutting down their web site and tracking down the religion's leadership and arresting them.[33] Since that time, the Chinese government has set up its own anti–Falun Gong site in an attempt to portray their side of the story.

Not only is Beijing using the Internet to quickly and efficiently disseminate its version of news and propaganda, but it is also attempting to use the web as a means to centralize control over many of the outlying provinces. China is currently working to streamline government bureaucracy in order to keep a tight control on the economy via better control of provincial taxation. They are doing this by creating a "government online" with the stated purpose of getting a majority of all government bodies on the Internet. Project goals include posting online government functions, duties, organizational structure, and administrative procedure, making available government documents and archives, and releasing the daily activities of government departments.[34] In this sense, China is attempting to subvert the Internet as a means to the solidification of Beijing's power.

What then has been the contemporary outcome of all these efforts by both the pro-democracy and pro-regime forces? Interestingly enough, the 2001 crisis between the United States and China over the downing of a U.S. EP-3 surveillance aircraft showed a Chinese populace that fell into line with the communist party view with regards to where the culpability of the incident lay. "The chat rooms have been full of anger towards the U.S.—but no one questions the official version of the collision or complains about the missile buildup against Taiwan that this plane was apparently monitoring."[35] This gets to the very crux of the issue, for if the majority of Chinese netizens simply do not question the government on an issue such as this, who is to say that these same people will pursue even greater goals like democratization?

Conclusion

What then does the future of the Internet hold for China? The deficiency of hard evidence pointing to an increase in mass demonstrations, public disillusionment, overt threats to the regime, or even the spread of democratic sympathies in China suggests that democratization in China, at least as instigated by the Internet, will not occur for some time. The CCP seems to be successfully promoting self-censorship among users, Internet service providers, and news agencies, while its police and judicial system make public examples of those who flagrantly refuse to adhere to the government-issued standards. At the same time, the rampant nationalism on the Internet that most demonstrated in April of 2001 seems to indicate that many young, educated, urban Internet users are more interested in Chinese greatness than any liberalization that may occur, a fact that plays directly into the hands of the totalitarians in Beijing.

It is sometimes forgotten that the Internet is a tool, nothing more. It is neither inherently good nor evil, benign nor malevolent. As such, what matters most is how it is used, and for as long as the Chinese government continues to be proficient at using the Internet to tighten its control over the populace, there is no reason to believe that an entire generation of Internet users will be conditioned to use the web in a manner beneficial to the democracy. Duncan Clark, managing director of Business Development Asia, a telecommunications industry consultant firm, points out that "the Internet has no value system. If Berlin had the Internet in 1935, I am sure people would have surfed nazi.gov."[36]

By the same token, it could be argued that Beijing would only successfully censor the Internet up to the point when usage outstrips the CCP's ability to police the web. However, with the unfathomable manpower resources of China, there is no reason why the CCP should not simply increase the number of "Internet police" at the same rate of the increasing users, at least for the foreseeable future.

There is therefore no reason to believe that the Internet will be the overriding causal factor in the democratization of China. Despite the hopes of many scholars, pundits, and political scientists in the West, the evidence for such an outcome does not exist. The Internet could conceivably empower a more organized attempt at overthrowing the CCP, but it will not bring about a mass change in values and ideals for which many have hoped. To once again quote Nina Hachigian, "in the near term, the Internet may in fact strengthen the party . . . The power shifts wrought by the Internet will suffice only during an economic or political crisis in a future China where the Internet is far more pervasive. At that time, the Internet will fuel discontent and could be a linchpin to a successful challenge to party rule."[37]

Notes

1. Bates Gill, "Technology, Pluralism and Regional Order: The Case of China," unpublished paper.
2. Larry Diamond and Ramon Myers, "Elections and Democracy in Greater China," *The China Quarterly* 162 (June 2000): 371.
3. Tedjabayu, "Indonesia: The Net as Weapon," *Cybersociology*, May 1, 2001, http://www.socio.demon.co.uk/mazazine/5/5indonesia.html.
4. Ibid.
5. Walter B. Wriston, "Bits, Bytes and Diplomacy," *Foreign Affairs* 76, no. 5 (Sept/Oct 1997): 172.
6. Ibid., p. 175.
7. Quoted in Rodar, "The Internet and Political Control in Singapore," *Singaporeans for Democracy*, March 1, 2001, http://www.gn.apc.org/sfd.
8. Ibid.
9. "Jiang Tough on Internet in '60 Minutes' Interview," *Virtual China*, May 1, 2001, http://www.virtualchina.com.
10. "Crackdown Time: Why Beijing Fears the Falun Gong," *National Review*, September 27, 1999.
11. Nina Hachigian, "China and the Net: A Love-Hate Relationship," *ChinaOnline*, March 15, 2001, http://www.chinaonline.com/commentary_analysis/internet/newsarchive/secure/2001/March/C01030160.asp.
12. Ibid.
13. Peter Weigang Lu, "Internet Development in China," *ChinaOnline*, April 1, 2001, http://www.chinaonline.com/commentary_analysis/internet/newsarchive/secure/2000/march/c00031601a2.asp.
14. John Daly, "Will the Internet Promote Democracy?" Center for Information Strategy and Policy, February 15, 2001, http://www.cisp.org/imp/september_2000/daly/09_00dayly.htm.
15. "China Drafts Law on Internet Based Crises," *ChinaOnline*, October 24, 2000, http://www.chinaonline.com/issues/internet_policy/newsarchives/secure/2000/october/c00102312.asp.
16. Ibid.
17. Shanthi Kalathi, "The Internet and Asia: Broad Band or Broad Bans?" *Foreign Service Journal* 78, no. 2 (February 2001), accessed February 25, 2001, http://www.ceip.org/files/publications/internet_asia.asp?.
18. Gill, "Technology."

19. "China's Print Media Concerned Over New Internet Portals," *ChinaOnline*, September 22, 1999, http://www.chinaonline.com/refer/legal/newsarchive/secure/1999/septermber/c9092180e-ss.asp.

20. The fact that these professionals understand that they are benefiting from the strict control of the PRC would make them hesitant to criticize the regime, for fear of being punished. This punishment could well result in the totalitarian CCP stripping them of the benefits and luxuries they have achieved during the past few years of economic growth, forcing them, in effect, to return to the peasant, subsistence-level incomes in which most Chinese find themselves. What the state gives, the state can take away.

21. "China Netizens Earn Above Average Salaries: Survey," *ChinaOnline*, April 2, 2001, http://www.chinaonline.com/issues/internet_policy/newsarchive/secure/2001/april/c01032905.asp.

22. Gill, "Technology."

23. "State Council Tightens Control Over Internet Cafes," *ChinaOnline*, April 17, 2001, http://www.chinaonline.com/issues/internet_policy/newsarchive/secure/2001/april/c01041201.asp.

24. Ibid.

25. "Going Offline: Guangdong's Fuoshon Closes Its Net Cafes," *ChinaOnline*, April 17, 2001, http://www.chinaonline.com/issues/social_political/newsarchive/secure/2000/september/c00092501.asp.

26. "Curses! Guangdong Firm Fined for Employee's Online Swearing," *ChinaOnline*, January 30, 2001, http://www.chinaonline.com/issues/internet_policy/newsarchives/secure/2001/january/c01012506.asp.

27. "Beijing Doubles Tax on Arcades, Internet Cafes," *ChinaOnline*, April 25, 2001, http://www.chinaonline.com/issues/internet_policy/currentnews/open/b100040521.asp.

28. Thomas Crampton, "Beijing Uses Cyberspace to Widen Control; Democracy via Internet for Chinese Is Stifled," *International Herald Tribune*, 24 March 2001.

29. Ibid.

30. Calum Macleod, "China's Internet Firms: Building a Bridge to Cross the River," *ChinaOnline*, April 19, 2001, http://www.chinaonline.com/issues/internet/policy/newsarchive/secure/2001/april/c01041957.asp.

31. "US Journalists Decry China's Imprisonment of Two Internet Writers," *Freedom Forum*, May 1, 2001, http://www.freedomforum.org/templates/document.asp?document1d=3003.

32. *Democracy.org*, May 1, 2001, http://www.democracy.org/hk/en/index.html.

33. Several dozen of whom have died while in custody.

34. Kalathi, "The Internet and Asia."

35. Mark O'Neill, "Anti-US Fervor Pours into Chat Rooms," *South China Morning Post*, 8 April 2001.

36. http://www.democracy.org/hk/en/index.html.

37. Hachigian, "China and the Net."

CHAPTER 9

The Internet and the Evolution of Civil Society in Iran

Michael J. Rabasco

The advent of the information revolution across the globe is having a profound effect on the way that people communicate, learn, wage war, and conduct commerce. Many high priests of the information revolution believe that—by improving the quality and reach of basic education, fostering critical scientific exchanges and medical advances, improving commerce, and facilitating low-cost global communication—these technologies have the power to transform societies. When we look to specific cases, however—cases such as Iran—the assumptions underlying these claims tend to wither.

Those assumptions are distantly related to the parallel assumptions of the "democratic peace theory," which contends that, because democracies do not wage war on one another, the promotion of democracy should be a primary foreign policy goal, and of "trade liberalization theory," which contends that trade binds states together and discourages conflict through economic interdependence. Although not as clearly articulated as these theories, what might be called an emerging "technoglobalization theory" suggests that telecommunications technology has the power to promote respect for human rights, foster transparency and the rule of law, and thereby foster freedom and democracy in closed, authoritarian societies.

Iran is a good test case of these notions. Over the past six years, an increasingly powerful reform movement has taken root in Iran, challenging the conservative stranglehold on power—and outside observers have begun to question whether the Internet has played a minor, critical, or causal role in this process. The answers—related to Iran and other countries—could have broad implications for U.S. foreign policy. If the Internet has the ability to influence such movements, then perhaps policymakers should refine U.S. export policy and retool existing sanction regimes in order to promote connectivity and, thereby, democracy and free trade.

The Wiring of the Islamic Republic

The degree of Iran's connectivity to the Internet is surprising. For a country that established its first Internet connection only in 1992, Iran had tens of thousands of users by 1999 and has often exhibited the highest growth rates in the Middle East.[1] As of 2000–2001 the country boasted between 450 and 1,200 cyber cafes.[2]

Iran has three highly reliable external Internet links: the Institute for Studies in Theoretical Physics & Mathematics (satellite via the Netherlands), Data Processing of Iran (DPI) (satellite via the Netherlands), and the Data Communication Company of Iran (DCI), which has three satellite links through Canada, Kuwait, and France.[3] While many of these connections are relatively slow, they are being regularly upgraded. Iran also has two fiber optic connections, one via an underwater Alcatel cable and the other through the Trans-Asia-Europe (TAE) line, which runs from France to China.[4]

The cost of the Internet is still rather high. The average cost for the use of a cafe is $3 per hour, and the annual cost of web page registration, reservation, and maintenance is approximately $50 after a one-time $100 domain registration cost.[5] Recent reports suggest that the rates have decreased to about $2 per hour,[6] down from 1999 figures suggesting that the average annual cost of Internet service for one hour per day was $330.[7] Aside from some content censorship and the somewhat high use costs, most people with enough money and a phone line can acquire access to the net.

More recent reports show that Internet usage is growing rapidly. It is estimated that today 400,000 Iranians have Internet accounts.[8] In addition, Iran's telecommunications infrastructure is expanding. To date, the Telecommunications Company of Iran (TCI) has laid 7,000 kilometers of fiber optic cable and plans to lay an additional 11,500 kilometers of cable within the next few years.[9] Iran is also rapidly expanding its fixed and mobile phone network; all of these developments in the telecom sector will increase bandwidth and increase Internet speed.[10] Sixty percent of the population is not only very young (25 and under) but is literate and highly educated. These demographic realities combined with Iran's positive IT growth could prove to be a powerful and explosive mixture for the future of domestic politics.

What the Mullahs Are Saying

In 2000 there were positive signals from Iran's leading politicians and institutions about the role and growth of the Internet. For example, NPR reported during the Majlis elections of 2000 that one mullah said of satellite receivers—officially banned but rarely confiscated—that "We should accept the reality of satellites and the Internet in peoples' homes."[11] The former president, member of Parliament, and chair of the Council of Guardians, Ali Hashemi Rafsanjani, admitted that "We cannot prevent computer and satellite networks on the pretext of safeguarding morality."[12] In May of 2000, Iranian state radio announced that, "steps have been taken so that the entire population can use Internet services around the country."[13] These statements are a testament to the fact that Iranians increasingly are going online and that the leadership is recognizing its social and political significance.

Over the past few years Internet Service Providers (ISPs) have flourished in Iran with at least 100 in existence as of late 2001.[14] These ISPs offer a range of e-mail, use-net and web-site hosting and design services. Until the summer of 2001, the Internet seemed relatively free of restrictions; some cyber cafes voluntarily blocked access to certain "objectionable" Internet sites—for example, one cafe in Tehran requires all Internet users fill out a form with their personal information and sign a pledge stating, "I will respect the laws of the Islamic Republic of Iran"[15]—but official policy was lenient.

During 2001, this approach began to change, and the ruling clerics issued several formal restrictions on Internet use. Between May and June 2001, the TCI shut down approximately 450 cyber cafes in Tehran on the charge that they lacked the appropriate permits. However, no such permits existed, and most were allowed to reopen after paying a registration fee to TCI.[16] Many Iranians were using Voice Over Internet Protocols to make inexpensive long-distance phone calls; in other words, TCI was losing revenue, and it is possible that the policy was not political in nature but rather motivated by financial concerns.

In June 2001, however, TCI issued a formal set of regulations for Internet use. It ordered all ISPs to block immoral, pornographic sites, in addition to those deemed a threat to national security.[17] Previously, TCI simply strongly suggested that ISPs block these sites. *Hambastegi,* a daily newspaper, reported that TCI also prohibited cyber cafes from allowing those under 18 to use the Internet. However, TCI rejected these claims and stated that it only banned youth from "owning" such cafes.[18]

The status of this regulation is still in question. More restrictions seem in the offing: The Minister of Post, Telegraph & Telephone, Ahmad Motamedi, recently stated that he sent a package of Internet regulations to President Khatami for review and that the government would soon install filters to block inappropriate material.[19] In November of 2001, the Supreme Council for Cultural Revolution issued a decree ordering all ISPs to offer Internet service through TCI by May of 2002.[20] The Voice of America (RFE/RFL) reported on March 25, 2002, that TCI cut Internet access to private sector ISPs in accord with these new regulations. However, this report also noted that local media outlets claimed that these regulations were being unevenly enforced. The Internet Networks Employers Guild sent a letter to President Khatami to protest these regulations (Khatami supported the new rules) and asked him to either repeal or amend them.[21] It is uncertain whether or not these restrictive Internet regulations will be realized. The reformist Majlis may intervene, because this decree is contrary to a move that would begin permitting foreign investment in and privatization of mobile and fixed-line telecommunications. These anticipated regulatory changes also include allowing foreign investment in Internet access networks.

Dr. Payman Arabshahi, an expert on the telecom sector in Iran and a researcher for NASA's Jet Propulsion Laboratory, said in a recent interview that "web page content monitoring is not easily regulated. Although all ISPs in Iran do provide web hosting for their users, many users choose to use free web hosting services abroad . . . So as long as you can get on the Net, you can pretty much do whatever you want, including setting up web pages outside Iran, or surfing to any sites that may be 'blocked' using a variety of proxy and/or anonymizing services (e.g. safeweb.com)."[22]

Initially, the Internet was not deemed a threat to the ruling establishment as its costs were high and access was very limited. However, even the conservative mullahs have recognized the potential security threat the large growth rates of Internet access and the proliferation of cyber cafes and computers pose to their regime. Accordingly, they are just beginning to implement formal policies to control web-page content and block objectionable web sites. However, given the nature of the technology, they will not be successful in completely controlling Internet content and access in Iran.

Democracy Via the Internet?

When considering the current and potential impact of the Internet in Iran, it is important to keep in mind that, unlike many other authoritarian states, Iran retains traces of an activist civil society—one that advocated varying degrees of pluralism and self-determination throughout its history. That history is rife with instances where a highly motivated and influential civil society protested for change. Even within the walls of the Shi'ite *madresehs* (religious seminaries) the tradition of debate, rhetoric, and respect for differing interpretations of Islam still exists despite the revolution's politicalization of the clergy and its absolutist interpretation of Islam.

Dr. Shaul Bakhash, a prominent scholar on modern Iranian politics and history, remarked in a recent interview that

> In recent Iranian history there have been repeated occurrences of mass political movements . . . I think history would indicate that there is the [recurring] potential . . . for the organization of mass political movements on . . . issues of nationalism and religion or protests against the government . . . on one level the potential for civil society is so vigorous and at another level so unable to endure.[23]

Iran may therefore be an especially promising test case of whether, and how, the Internet might promote democracy in closed societies. In particular, we have the opportunity to examine the specific role of the Internet in a recent, and still ongoing, period of change: Iran's "Fourth Wave" of reform.

Since the death of Ayatollah Khomeini in 1989, the ruling clergy has attempted to moderate its foreign policy, reform Iran's anemic economy, stabilize the states along its borders, and begin the slow process of rebuilding and modernizing the state. The stagnant economy and increasingly strict social restrictions created discontent in Iran's educated and youthful population and gave rise to the Fourth Wave in the mid 1990s. The widely used term "reformer" is actually a blanket term used to identify a myriad of groups with differing agendas, all of which oppose the regime for various reasons. Although the conservatives control the radio and television, independent newspapers expressing alternative views have flourished since the election of President Mohammad Khatami. Similarly, political and civic organizations have appeared despite the fact that political parties are technically illegal. Riots have even erupted in major cities in response to alleged corruption and the strict Islamic social codes still in force.

On May 23, 1997, the people elected Mohammed Khatami, a moderate mullah, as the President of the Islamic Republic of Iran with 70 percent of the vote. Turnout was heavy; eighty percent of the voting age populace cast ballots. Similarly, a large majority of the eligible population voted in the February 18, 2000 election of the Sixth Majlis in which "reformers" or "moderates" gained about 75 percent of the 290 seats. The perceived importance and the increasing accessibility of the Internet was apparent as both candidates had their own web sites (www.khatami.com and www.nateq.co.ir) espousing their respective agendas.

The Internet and Iranian Politics

Although Internet-use levels are much lower in Iran than in most Western states, the country is a leader in Net access in the Middle East. Iranians are flocking online: As Internet cafes boom in Tehran and in all Iran's major cities, and as more cities are wired, a worldwide network of information is reaching into the far corners of Persia. The Internet is being used to send e-mail; download college applications, music, and videos; obtain news; and do dozens of other things. Iranians have broad access to independent, international news broadcasts.[24] A recent poll of students conducted by Iran's Public Opinion Department found that they use the Internet "primarily for research and data purposes, followed by information and news, entertainment, and mail and communication."[25] In a state where the media is tightly controlled by the regime, the Internet is becoming an increasingly important factor in public discourse and a source of outside information regarding politics, culture, and economics.

It appears that most governmental and political entities have an Internet presence, the most significant of which are: the largest reformist party at www.jebhemosharekat.com; President Khatami at www.gov.ir/; the reformist parliament at www.majlis.ir/; a site for the recent June 8, 2001 presidential election at www.entekhab80.20m.com; an active student group at Amir Kabir Technical University at www.akunews.com; the largest conservative party at www.mesbahyazdi.org/; and the Supreme Leader Ayatollah Khameini at www.wilayah.org. All of these sites are in Farsi.

One estimate suggests the existence of approximately 1,500 Iranian web sites devoted to politics, society, and culture, 300 of which are expressly political in nature.[26] The presence of these political sites may hint at the growing perceived importance of establishing an online presence to establish political legitimacy. The latest Internet statistics come from the Iranian daily *Hambastegi* (online in Farsi), which reported a total of 418,000 Iranian Internet users between 2000–2001 and projected 1.326 million by 2001–2002.[27] These reports also suggest that the cost of service has been reduced dramatically due to competition among the 100 ISPs.[28]

The importance of the new medium is now widely recognized. Dr. Assad Homayoun, the President of Azedagan, an Iranian exile organization, has argued that "Mao Tse-Tung used to say that real power emanated from the barrel of a gun, but today real power comes from the Internet."[29] While Dr. Homayoun's enthusiasm for the power of the Internet may be slightly exaggerated, Iran is changing with the help of the Internet. For example, Nasser Hadian-Jazy, a political science professor at the University of Tehran, concurs that, "like it or not, the satellite and the Internet are changing Iran and the conservatives have no idea how to deal with it."[30]

Christiane Amanpour of CNN has argued that "press analysis of the election testif[ies] to the importance of local and global networks in rallying political opposition and raising money."[31] In a recent interview, Dr. Payman Arabshahi echoed these remarks and stated that the Internet was used to help organize the opposition.[32] *The Vancouver Sun* reported that two factors led to Khatami's election: displeasure with the ruling conservatives, and the opposition's ability to "effectively network through liberal media outlets," which included "proliferating web sites."[33]

The Conservatives Fight Back

The trend toward reform and openness, and the Internet's growing role in that trend, has not escaped the notice of forces opposed to change; and since the reformist Majlis victory in 2000, the conservatives have counterattacked. Using the courts, security services, and the "morals police," they cracked down on the reformers and began to close

newspapers and fine and imprison their respective editors and reporters. The intensity of the press crackdown increased in early 2001 when
the conservatives began jailing and arresting reformist activists and
many of President Khatami's supporters. As of April 2001, 53 reformist
newspapers were closed.[34] It appears this crackdown was an attempt to
prevent Khatami's supporters from organizing rallies and critical "get-
out-the-vote" activities for the June 8, 2001, presidential election.
However, Khatami won a surprising 77 percent of the popular vote, an
8 percent increase over his margin of victory in 1997. Whether or not he
can use this momentum to jump start his anemic reform program is
uncertain at best.

Reformist groups have used the Internet to help blunt the effects of
this assault. In response to this media crackdown a site was established,
www.payvand.com, that is dedicated to promoting freedom of the
press in Iran. This site urges readers to mail or e-mail protest form
letters to any of the several addresses provided. Although it is based in
California, it enables Iranians to voice their protests relatively easily. In
addition, it lists all the conservative newspapers still operational and
dozens of reformist papers that have been banned. Of the 19 major
reformist newspapers that have corresponding web sites, 10 are still in
operation. No evidence indicates that the government has shut any of
these sites down. As Dr. Arabshahi has commented, "the government
has not shown an inclination to shut down Internet sites of papers,
especially since many of these sites are 'physically' located outside Iran.
Many sites have, however, expired, and are no longer accessible. Or the
webmaster has simply gone away, and the site is no longer maintained."[35]

As the political debate becomes increasingly polarized, the reformers
may come to rely primarily, if not exclusively, on the Internet to
promote their agenda and organize their political activities. A journalist, Ali Hekmat, recently argued that "Everyone else knows that, when
a newspaper is closed, there is still satellite television, the Internet and
books."[36] This is a medium that is rapidly becoming a threat to the
conservatives. An anonymous student at a Tehran Internet cafe wrote
that "They took those newspapers off the streets, but we can still get the
news we want from the Internet."[37]

It is no surprise, then, that the rapid growth of the Internet has
alarmed the ruling clergy, and they are now imposing a series of
restrictions on its use. Ayatollah Mesbah Yazdi, a prominent hardliner,
argued that "We are facing a veritable cultural invasion. Our enemies
are unable to send soldiers to fight us. So they are lulling us into
cyberspace where we will be forced to fight on their terms."[38] Several
religious leaders and conservative parties have posted their own web

sites and are fighting back by promoting their own content. One report indicates that virtually all theology students use the Internet.[39]

The Grand Ayatollah of Cyberspace

Perhaps the most significant and concrete example of the powerful effects of the Internet rests with the frail, 79-year-old cleric, Grand Ayatollah Hussein Ali Montazeri. Montazeri is one of the most influential religious leaders in Iran and within the entire Shi'ia faith. He was one of the architects of the revolution, helped draft the Constitution of 1979, and was Ayatollah Khomeini's chosen successor. However, shortly before Khomeini's death in 1989, Montazeri fell out of favor with Khomeini. Subsequently, he was publicly derided and shunned by the ruling elite. Since 1989 he has been an outspoken critic of the regime and the role of the clergy in the state. Montazeri does not seek to completely eliminate Islam from the state but rather believes the clergy should play an advisory role and leave all other matters of state to the elected officials. He opposed Khomeini's hardline tactics, believing that the role of the Supreme Leader *(velayat-e faqih)* was only a supervisory position and not one that controlled the levers of power.[40] He was finally arrested and placed under house arrest in 1997. His incendiary remarks sparked massive pro- and anti-Montazeri riots in the spring of 1998.

Under constant police guard, confined to his house, Montazeri's only contact with the outside world was his family, especially his two sons.[41] However, this dramatically changed last year. Through his single phone line, Montazeri established a United Kingdom–based web site (www.montazeri.com) with the help of his two sons. This site posts Montazeri's teachings and political speeches and contains dozens of photos of him in different settings and with prominent Iranian officials. The most shocking event came when Montazeri posted 700 pages of his memoirs online in early December 2000.[42] In these pages he speaks about the unjust execution of thousands of innocent civilians and helpless prisoners during the revolution. He also names those responsible. In addition, he explains how he opposed sending teenagers to the front lines during the Iran-Iraq war and how the regime made a grave error by not ending the Iran-Iraq war in 1982.[43] The day after the memoirs were posted on the site, a countersite appeared claiming to be the real site at www.montazery.com.[44] In addition, the British Broadcasting Service reported that Montazeri's site was offline due to a deliberate cyber attack by the regime.[45] Despite some interruption, the site remains online to this day (although it is now located at a_h_a_montazeri@yahoo.com) and has registered over 410,000 hits. One supporter stated, "Maybe technology has finally given him the freedom he has been denied for nearly three decades."[46] According to Dr. Arabshahi, the stinging revelations exposed in Montazeri's memoirs have been the most popular topic in Iran over the last few months.[47]

On April 27, 2001, I sent Montazeri a brief e-mail asking his thoughts about the importance of the Internet in Iran. The following form letter reply was received in English:

> In the name of God. Dear Brother and Sister. On account of the unlawful arrest of the reverend jurist and religious leader Ayatollah Aluzma Montazeri, questions and messages received, are submitted to His Highness through an intermediary. Hence, some delay naturally takes place in dispatch of replies. God willing, it is our aspiration to see this blatant injustice and illegal-dastardly house-arrest removed and the opportunity reestablished for direct contact with His Highness.[48]

Apparently, his sons download the messages, organize them by topic, and Montazeri replies.[49]

In this case, the Internet empowered Montazeri to overcome his physical imprisonment and circumvent his state-imposed censorship. In using the Internet, he was able to publish his controversial memoirs, which have shocked and embarrassed the hardliners. Newspapers reporting his memoirs have been closed, reporters jailed, and even one of his sons was imprisoned for distributing sections of the memoirs. However, his site is still online and his memoirs are still available.

Student Protest Movements

A second case deals with the use of the Internet by Iran's traditionally restive university students. Student-run organizations played an important role in the election of Khatami in 1997 and 2001. The students are educated, young, politically aware, and a large number of them are advocating for major domestic reforms and increased social freedom.

Two recent events in particular provoked these student organizations. First, Ali Afshari, a prominent student organizer and secretary of the Organization to Foster Unity (an umbrella organization for various university political groups), was arrested on December 17, 2000, for delivering a speech at Amir Kabir Technical University calling for drastic government reform; he has since disappeared.[50] Second, seven reformists were arrested, convicted, and jailed for attending an October 2000 conference in Berlin regarding the prospects for reform in Iran.[51]

Prompted by these two acts, along with the assault on the reformist press that resulted in dozens of newspaper closures, the students of Amir Kabir Technical University (AKU) began to protest online. AKU's Islamic Association of Students announced that its web site could be used by Iranians to talk to students about their political views.[52] Dr. Arabshahi, who has surveyed these news reports and their sites in Farsi, argues that

> All Iranian universities have these associations. Over the past few years these groups have increasingly become political, issuing communiques, and organizing campus speeches by reformist personalities.
>
> The AKU [Amir Kabir Technical University] student group is perhaps the most "Internet" enabled group. They recently launched their own web site (www.akunews.com), and . . . they have an active yahoo club. Issues discussed are 99% political, and these days especially, about the election, and tactics used by both camps. News of campus events are publicized in advance on the site, and the site and the club are used to disseminate views of the group, as well as "underground" or little heard of letters or protests by other people (notably families of people and journalists jailed).[53]

Another student protest site was established at http://www.iran-daneshjoo.com, with both English and Farsi versions. This site has information about the arrest and harassment of activists, news reports, and an "urgent action" section. It also contains a section entitled "Schedule of Demonstrations," apparently a portal through which students can organize their political activities. The site lists specific details about each demonstration (time, date, form of protest, the issue, the speaker, etc. . . .) in cities throughout Iran. This site also organizes international protests (mostly in Europe), which demonstrates that these students are using both domestic and international networks to garner support.

As an example of the protests made possible by such technologies, on February 10, 2001, at 12:00 P.M., this site called for a coordinated protest at 13 different locations throughout Iran (3 were in Tehran). While the results of this event are unknown, the Internet has provided these individuals a means of organization never before available. The Internet is a critical tool with which these "Internet enabled" students protest government actions, propagate their agenda, organize their activities, and support their candidates. Net politics in Iran are still nascent but are growing at a fast pace and will likely play an increasingly important role in the evolution of the domestic reform movement.

The Internet as Catalyst for Reform

These cases demonstrate that the Internet has played an important role in the development of the Fourth Wave of reform in Iran. It is also true that the Internet is flourishing in Iran *because* of this movement: The highly literate and young reformers are increasingly utilizing the tools of the Internet to promote their agendas, organize, and circumscribe the conservative stranglehold on radio, television, and the print media. Not only are the several reformist newspapers continuing their struggle online, but student political organizations and dissidents such as Ayatollah Montazeri are taking their fight to cyberspace. Through the Internet, Montazeri has shaken the clerical establishment. They are attempting to fight back by arresting anyone who is caught with a hard copy of his memoirs, but people are still free to read them online in their homes or when sipping tea in one of Tehran's 400-plus cyber cafes.

The Internet's unique empowering tools have given Iran's Fourth Wave a powerful new medium with which to achieve its goals. Iran has a proven history of vibrant civil society and activism—the Internet did not create these trends, but it has unquestionably empowered civil society. Dr. Arabshahi recognizes that the influence runs both ways when he comments that "Widespread Internet use has been both an effect of the movement, and a source of contribution to its rise."[54] John Daly agrees that "The Internet complements mass media, and potentially gives people who could never use radio or television to disseminate their views an electronic medium by which to do so."[55]

The Internet is truly revolutionizing Iran's reform movement and is an increasingly important factor in the domestic struggle for power. No other example better demonstrates the unique nature of the Internet than the following: On May 5 and July 15, 2001, Ayatollah Montazeri (an architect of the Islamic revolution, a confidant to and former successor to Ayatollah Khomeini), from house arrest in the Shi'ite religious center of Qom, reached across cyberspace to send the following two e-mails about the Internet in the form of scanned gif. files:

> In the name of God. With Greetings and thanks. Common sense requires human beings to make use, with their utmost power, all the world's advanced means, ways and devices to achieve their legitimate goals. And,

this is evidence of being grateful to God. I wish you all success, (Signet Stamp of Ayatollah Montazeri).[56]

In a follow up to this response Montazeri wrote after the June presidential election that:

Students more or less have used the Internet and they use it today. Every wise human being should use the possibilities and innovation for his own legitimate objections. Unfortunately, my site has been vandalized during the past few days. In the same way that the Internet is used for righteousness and goodness, wicked people also use it, but to further their corruption (Signet Stamp of Ayatollah Montazeri).[57]

The students and this dissident Ayatollah are using the Internet to access outside information and to engage the ruling establishment politically. The Internet is a form of communication that is fundamentally altering the manner in which people communicate and acquire, possess, and distribute information. Montazeri succinctly captured the dilemma this empowering technology poses to society: The Internet can be used as a means for both good and bad. Given the changes occurring in Iran, it is too early to tell how this competition will unfold.

Notes

1. Dr. Payman Arabshahi, "Iran's Telecom & Internet Sector: A Comprehensive Survey of the Internet in Iran," Open Research Network, June 15, 1999, p. 1–2, http://www.science-arts.org/internet.
2. "Iran: Internet-Logging On," *Economist Intelligence Unit,* July 16, 2001, http://www.eiu.com.
3. Arabshahi, "Iran's Telecom & Internet Sector," sec. 2.3.
4. Ibid., sec. 3.2.1.2.
5. Ibid., sec.4.1.1.6.
6. Molly Moore, "Cybermania Takes Iran by Surprise; Youths Swarm Online; Tehran Scrambles to Respond," July 4, 2001, http://www.washingtonpost.com.
7. Douglas Jehl, "The Internet's 'Open Sesame' Is Answered Warily," March 18, 1999, http://www.nyt.com.
8. Amir Taheri, "Internet Becomes a Battlefield in Iran," *Middle East Newsfile,* March 2001.
9. "Special Report on Iran Telecoms," *Middle East Economic Digest,* August 24, 2001.
10. Ibid.
11. "Scott Simon and Jennifer Ludden, "Iranian Parliamentary Elections," National Public Radio transcript, February 18, 2000, http://www.nationalpublicradio.org.
12. "Iran Hard-liners Reinvent Themselves," Associated Press Online, January 31, 2000, http://www.ap.org.

13. "Websurfing in Iran," *IPR Strategic Business Information Database*, Info-Prod Research: Middle East, May 17, 2000.
14. "Special Report on Iran Telecoms."
15. Ibid.
16. "Iran: Internet-Logging On."
17. "Iran Imposes New Rules on Internet Use," *National Journal's Technology Daily*, June 25, 2001.
18. "MP Urges Government to Recognize Youth's Right to Access," *BBC Worldwide Monitoring*, June 28, 2001.
19. Moore, "Cybermania Takes Iran By Surprise."
20. Firouz Sederat, "Iran Move to Monopolize Internet Access Draws Fire," November 14, 2001, http:www.Infowar.com.
21. "Iran: Internet Providers Protest New Regulations," *Financial Times*, Global News Wire, April 22, 2002.
22. Dr. Payman Arabshahi interview via e-mail with the author, April 27-May 2, 2001. Dr. Arabshahi is the author of a comprehensive survey on Iran's telecom sector, a researcher with NASA's Jet Propulsion Laboratory, and an associate professor at the University of Washington.
23. Dr. Shaul Bakhash interview via telephone with the author, May 3, 2001. Dr. Bakhash is a professor at George Mason University, author of several books and articles on Iran, and a preeminent scholar on Iranian history, domestic affairs, and politics.
24. "Websurfing in Iran."
25. "Internet Poll Taken in Iran," *Info-Prod Research Strategic Business Information Database*, July 5, 2001.
26. Taheri, "Internet Becomes a Battlefield in Iran."
27. *Hambastegi*, an Iranian print daily (www.hambastegi-news.com). The article was located and translated by Dr. Payman Arabshahi and conveyed to the author via e-mail, May 6, 2001.
28. Ibid.
29. "Iran's Progress Masks Continuing Polarization," *Defense and Foreign Affairs Strategic Policy* 28, no. 5 (May 2002): p. 20.
30. Tom Hundley, "At Tehran Burger They Serve Sides of Piping Hot Reform," *The Chicago Tribune*, 30 July 2000.
31. Christiane Amanpour, "Revolutionary Journey," CNN Perspectives, February 27, 2000.
32. Arabshahi interview.
33. Amyn Sajoo, "Factions Fight for Iran's Future," *The Vancouver Sun*, 24 July 1999.
34. Taheri, "Internet Becomes a Battlefield in Iran."
35. Arabshahi interview.
36. Hundly, "At Tehran Burger."
37. "Trendy Cafes Open Window to the World," *The Washington Times*, 17 May 2000.
38. Taheri, "Internet Becomes a Battlefield in Iran."
39. Ibid.
40. Patrick Clawson, Michael Eisenstadt, et al., *Iran Under Khatami* (Washington, DC: The Washington Institute for Near East Policy, 1998), p. 35.
41. Geneive Abdo, "In Iran, the Struggle to Define 'Islamic Republic,'" *International Herald Tribune*, 13 April 2001.
42. Agence France-Presse, "Iranian Cleric Goes to Battle in Cyberspace," December 17, 2000, http://www.nyt.com.

43. Abdo, "In Iran, Struggle to Define 'Islamic Republic.'"
44. Ibid.
45. British Broadcasting Corporation, "Iranian Authorities Said to Be Jamming Dissident Ayatollah's Website," December 24, 2000.
46. Geneive Abdo, "Online Ayatollah: Isolated Iranian Dissident Speaks Out on Web," *International Herald Tribune,* 17 December 2000.
47. Arabshahi interview.
48. E-mail from www.montazeri.com to the author, April 28, 2001.
49. Geneive Abdo, "Cyberspace Frees Iran's Rebel Cleric," *The Guardian,* 5 August 2000.
50. Amnesty International, "Urgent Action Appeal," December 18, 2000, http://www.amnesty-usa.org/urgent/action/iran10300_12182000.html.
51. "Iran Hands Stiff Sentences To Reformists," *The New York Times,* 14 January 2001.
52. BBC World Broadcasting Summaries, "Students Protesting against Court Verdict Make Historic Use of the Internet," *Hayat-e Now,* Tehran, January 24, 2001, http://www.aria.ws.hayateno.
53. Arabshahi Interview.
54. Arabshahi Interview.
55. John A. Daly, "Will the Internet Promote Democracy," *Information Impacts Magazine* (September 2000): 2.
56. Two emails from montazeri.com. The scanned files were translated by Manouchehr Kouchak, an English-Farsi language instructor at the Iranian Community School in Vienna, Virginia. Mr. Kouchak, a resident of Iran until 1985, believes that the Montazeri e-mails are legitimate as Ayatollahs only use their signet stamp on authentic documents.
57. Ibid.

PART THREE

The Internet and Economic Development

CHAPTER 10

From Tea Sheds to Cyber Cafes: Could an Internet-Driven Modernization Strategy Succeed in India?

Sudhir Mahara

India exhibits the ghastly extremes of a modernizing society, as did many other nations throughout history at its stage of development. Like Matthew Arnold's metaphor in the poem "Grande Chartreuse"— "Wandering between two worlds—one dead, the other powerless to be born"—India is caught between two realities. On the one hand, India is plagued by multiple insurrections, civil strife, and corruption.[1] Of its population of over 1 billion people, 44 percent are illiterate, 36 percent live under the poverty line, and 81 percent have access to "improved water source" (meaning that those implicated in this statistics cannot be classified as having access to totally safe drinking water).[2] Using the international poverty line as a guide, India is home to an estimated 40 percent of the world's poor. Public health continues to affect development: Half of all children under the age of four are malnourished; 60 percent of women are anemic; HIV/AIDS infections double every 14 months; and in absolute numbers India has the largest HIV population in the world.[3]

On the other hand, India shows all the promising signs of a rising and affluent power. Its GDP growth in 1995 was 7.7 percent, 6.8 percent in 1998, and 6.5 percent in 1999, demonstrating a steady average of 7 percent GDP growth.[4] In geopolitical terms, India's influence in the Indian Ocean and Asia Pacific is increasing, as is its nuclear capability.[5] In the words of Stephen Cohen, a senior fellow and South Asia analyst at the Brookings Institution, "historically, India has been the object of American charity and rarely viewed as part of Washington's strategy," but that perception is changing and for good reasons, both geopolitical and geoeconomic. India and Pakistan have recently tested nuclear weapons, and China, heavily involved in the South Asian security triangle, is known to have a nuclear arsenal.[6] India has a substantial and growing foothold in the software industry (for example, 60 percent of Bangalore's software is exported to the United States).[7] More broadly, South Asia analysts generally agree that, within a few decades, India will become a major player in international politics.[8]

The role of the Internet in India's emergence has not been widely discussed, but the technology could play a crucial role in India's transition from a developing to industrialized country. The Indian government, cognizant of the Internet's potential, is pursuing aggressive strategies to develop its Internet use and the health and growth of its information technology (IT) sector.[9] Recent policy decisions, in fact, indicate that the Indian government views the Internet and IT sector to be a major driver of its "modernization and development agenda."[10]

The question—for Indian government officials, outside aid agencies, and foreign donors trying to bring economic opportunity to India—is whether such a strategy is sound, given the primacy of other socioeconomic variables in India. In a situation as mixed and challenging as India's, is an Internet/IT-based development model a viable substitute for traditional models of development?[11]

India and the Indian IT Industry

The Indian economy in 1991 was in shambles. India's foreign debt was $70 billion and its foreign reserves barely covered two weeks of imports. Unemployment had reached 37.1 million and inflation was hovering at 14 percent. The account deficit was dangerously high, as 30 percent of export earnings were used to service foreign debt.[12]

After the assassination of the then–Prime Minister Rajiv Gandhi and the interim government of V. P. Singh, P. V. Narasimha Rao took the mantle of head of government. Soon after coming to power, Prime Minister Rao and his politically savvy finance minister Manmohan Singh took steps to liberalize the Indian economy.[13] Import duties, taxes, and red tape were cut, real market competition was introduced, and the barriers to foreign investment lifted. The door for foreign direct investment (FDI) opened after 1991.[14] The FDI inflow from January 1991 to December 2000 was $23.6 billion.[15] The "automatic approval mechanism" adopted by the government to speed the investment process ameliorated the investors' climate.[16]

As a result of specified Internet- and IT-related policies as well as general liberalization of the Indian economy, India's IT industry grew exponentially. During the period from 1999 to 2000, the IT industry earned an estimated $8.7 billion, an increase of 49.6 percent from 1998 to 1999, and growth rates were expected to remain above 50 percent for the foreseeable future.[17] India's IT advocates cite the success of one especially fast-growing region—Bangalore—as evidence that a technology-led development plan can work in the country.

The Story of Bangalore: What Made IT?

Bangalore is the capital of the state of Karnataka. It is the fifth largest city in India, with over 6 million people, and is the fastest growing city in all of Asia.[18] Texas Instruments built the first IT industry in the city in the early 1980s, and since then the massive growth of technology industry in the city has earned it the pseudonym "The New Silicon Valley."[19] Many factors inherent to the city, along with favorable government and private sector initiatives, contributed to Bangalore's success. One especially important factor is socioeconomic characteristics: The work force is highly skilled, efficient, and abundant, something that is the product of both colonialism and more modern circumstances. For example, the British introduced an English language–based educational system throughout India in order to produce indigenous civil servants to run a large bureaucracy. A large number of British schools were located close to Bangalore, primarily in order to take advantage of its temperate climate.

The city also benefited from an earlier, not always successful wave of IT investment: Companies like IBM opened facilities in the area and closed them by the early 1980s, leaving behind a cadre of technicians who became the nucleus of the first Indian IT industry. In early 1980,

Bangalore was selected as an industrial site by Texas Instruments, which trained a generation of Indian workers who joined the skilled workers already in place.

As a result, the city now has a reputation for providing superior education. Bangalore's literacy rate is 81 percent, a figure that starkly contrasts with the national average of 44 percent. Bangalore's physical infrastructure is not as advanced as in the United States or East Asia, but the city has an ample power supply, efficient transportation, and sophisticated communications—most importantly, bandwidth arrangements that provide ample access to the Internet. There are over 20 international carriers in operation with around 35 Megabit per second (Mb/s) direct connections to earth stations operating with IntelSat 64, over 140 radio installations, reliable data communications, and various international gateways.

Strange as it may seem, Bangalore's location in relation to the time difference to North America (9 to 12 hours ahead) is also a key factor in the growth of its service industry. As a senior manager in a U.S. IT industry puts it, "Bangalore works while we sleep." This advantage has been magnified by the Internet, which makes it possible for projects to be sent rapidly and cheaply back and forth between the United States and India. Industrial studies in the United States indicate that operating an IT industry in Bangalore costs about one-sixth to one-fifth of the cost in the United States and 30 to 40 percent less than in Southeast Asia.[20] Numbers like these have encouraged many international firms to outsource information technology projects to Indian companies.

India also benefits from having the second largest English-speaking manpower base in the world. In an international business environment where national borders are increasingly less significant, proficiency in English is fundamental, especially in the service sector. Given the advantage of language, workers in India are able to electronically provide services such as customer support to the services-hungry U.S. market.[21] Thus the combination of an established infrastructure, an educated and skilled work force, a central location, a temperate climate, and, of late, an accommodating state government, has made the city attractive for IT investors.

It would be tempting to believe that the Bangalore experience can be replicated throughout India, that this one case demonstrates the viability of an Internet- and IT-led development process. But the assumption that the same conditions can be recreated in other cities is fundamentally flawed. First, the advantage of early entry enjoyed by Bangalore's initial investors is no longer applicable. Second, many key socioeconomic characteristics like literacy rate, infrastructure, and political stability turn out to be unique to Bangalore. Third, two significant (and again unique) events contributed to Bangalore's discovery: the departure of IBM in 1978 and the selection of Bangalore as an industrial site by Texas Instruments in 1980.[22] And, finally, geographic conditions such as Bangalore's moderate climate and its central location in relation to other major cities in India may be impossible to duplicate.

Despite these facts, the Indian government seems to support the widely held assumption that the Bangalore miracle can be recreated. This is demonstrated in the aggressive policies it has announced in the last few years—policies that, if Bangalore is indeed a unique rather than precedent-setting case, seem destined to fail.

Ninth Five-Year Plan (1997–2002)[23]

At the national level, the impetus of the Indian government's development strategy is given by Five-Year Plans (FYP), which is devised by a National Planning Commission. According to the ninth FYP, a National Information Infrastructure (NII), a network of nationwide computer networks, is being formed. The Department of Telecommunications is strengthening the existing 40,000 km route of fiber optics to 1,000,000. The addition of over 100 mbps of external gateway capacity for linkages is expected to spawn an estimated 5,000 small and medium scale knowledge-based enterprises. In addition, every project in the states that is sponsored by the central government is required to utilize 3 percent of its total budget for information technology.

Information Technology Action Plan (ITAP)[24]

A national Task Force on Information Technology and Software Development submitted its report to the Indian government on July 4, 1998. The report recommended 108 "Action Points" to make India a global IT power. The recommendations covered a wide spectrum of issues relating to telecom, finance, banking, revenue, commerce, electronics, human resources development, defense, and rural development.

The ITAP maintains that India should aim at an annual export target in excess of U.S. $50 billion for computer software and U.S. $10 billion for computer and telecom hardware by the year 2008. The ITAP also proposes an "operation knowledge" campaign to spread IT culture throughout India. The policy framework and industrial strategy has been designed to comply with the demand of the World Trade Organization-Information Technology Agreement zero duty regime. According to ITAP, every secondary school and university library ought to be given computer and Internet access by 2003. The ITAP also proposes comprehensive measures to create a policy ambiance and investment climate comparable to those in Taiwan, Malaysia, and Singapore. In short, the ITAP seeks to replicate the success story of Bangalore in other states of India.[25]

The IT Bill for India 1999[26]
The clearance of the IT bill by the Indian cabinet soon after its formation is a major step toward creating a conducive environment for IT trade and e-commerce. The bill uses the UNICITRAL's (United Nations Commission on International Trade Law) Model Law on e-commerce; specifically, it: (1) gives legal validity to electronic contracts; (2) provides a system for authentication and identification of electronic documents; (3) calls for a tribunal to settle disputes; (4) contains stringent provisions for computer crimes, and; (5) amends existing regulations.

The Mahithi Initiative[27]
At the state level, the latest in Bangalore's IT policy is the Mahithi—the millennium IT policy for the state of Karnataka. The policy initiative was undertaken to manage an IT sector that has been growing exponentially. The key objectives of the millennium IT policy are: (1) to reduce unemployment by absorbing the major share of youth in IT related industry; (2) use e-governance to make governance proactive and responsive, and; (3) to encourage business with non-English-speaking countries. In addition, the state government—in order to promote IT-related investments—reduced state taxes for IT industries, built infrastructures, eliminated red tape, established venture capitals for start-up businesses, simplified labor laws, and encouraged dot-com companies developing Business to Business (B2B) and Business to Client (B2C) transactions to make business more efficient.[28] Many of the other states in India have declared policies that seek to replicate the resulting model.

Research and Development[29]
Some measures were also taken to encourage the development and application of indigenous technology in its economic sector. To this end, the Research and Development Act of 1986 was amended by the Technology Development Board Act in 1996, with the effect of creating a government fund that "invested in equity capitals or gave soft loans to industrial concerns and other agencies attempting to develop and commercially apply indigenous technology."[30] One result is that the city of Bangalore alone houses 15 world-class IT research organizations

that specialize in fields ranging from satellites, defense, telecommunications, and astrophysics to artificial intelligence and robotics. Similarly, there are 123 reputed private Internet/IT-related training institutes in Bangalore.[31]

IT Education[32]

The demand for IT jobs in India is estimated to be 3 million by 2002. There are, however, some challenges in filling the gap between supply and demand. For example, there is an imbalance in the supply of qualified engineers to all parts of the country, as the facility for IT education is confined to developed areas. There is also disparity in the quality of education provided by different institutes. Moreover, there is a shortage of good tutors in the education sector because the wages in the IT industry are much higher.

Recent decisions by the government, then, point to an urgency in both the government as well as the private sector to capitalize on the once-frenzied Internet boom. Closer examination of the policy initiatives, especially in relation to the extent of Internet penetration, the sociocultural settings of the country, and the existing institutional framework of the government that regulates issues such as patent rights and enforcement of Internet related legislations, reveals that there is a considerable gap between the initiatives taken and prerequisites for launching such programs.

From Dhabas to Dot-Coms: How Far Has Internet Penetration Reached in India?[33]

In the West, "Internet" has become a household word. Charles Swett says, in describing its spread, that "The Internet has burst onto the national scene and is playing an increasingly important role in an ever-widening spectrum of activities involving an exponentially increasing number of people. It is now in the mainstream. Having a tangible effect on in the social, cultural, economic, and political lives of millions, the evolution of the Internet is taking it into roles completely unanticipated by its original designers. Rather than merely 'fitting in' to pre-existing social processes, the Internet is actually transforming the nature of the processes themselves."[34]

Can the same be said about India, or might the same thing be said several decades or so from now? Will it be embraced by the Indian society as readily as in advanced countries? To answer such questions we first need a sense of the extent of Internet penetration in the Indian society.

A survey conducted in January 2001 by the National Association of Software and Service Companies (Nasscom) on Internet usage trends in 68 cities/towns in India showed that Internet subscribers in India increased from a base of 1.7 million subscribers in November 1998 to 18 million by December 2000.[35] A large portion of this increase, however, came from government rather than private initiatives. The Nasscom survey revealed that more than 200 cities and towns in India have Internet connectivity. As of December 2000, India had a personal computer (PC) base of 5 million PCs, 3.7 million of which had Pentium or more advanced chips that could be effectively used for the Internet.[36] Surveys indicate that more than 80 percent of PCs purchased over the last year or two were bought primarily with Internet access in mind. An exploding Internet industry is emerging to serve the resulting need; more than 120 private Internet Service Providers (ISPs) seemed likely to be in business by March 2001. Indian business interest is peaking as well: Nearly all corporate offices that responded to the survey endorsed the Internet and electronic commerce as being an integral part of their corporate strategic framework for next year. Their survey also suggested that India's major cities accounted for 79 percent of Internet connections across the country.

The findings of the Nasscom survey could be used to paint an optimistic picture about the potential for Internet growth in India, but when measured against the hard realities of India's infrastructure, such conclusions would be misleading. For example, the number of telephone mainlines available per 1,000 people was only 26.5 in 1999, a fraction of similar figures in the developed world. India had 3.3 PCs per 1,000 people in the same year, and only two Internet hosts per 10,000 people.[37] These figures show that at this rate the Internet as a communication medium will take decades to dislodge radio, television, and print media as the primary source of mass communication in the country.

India's sociocultural calculus (which is not fully receptive to new ideas) also militates against the assumption made by Internet advocates that the technology can contribute to effective governance. The bulk of technological infrastructures—telephone lines, power supplies, Internet hosts—required to operate the Internet are concentrated in the cities, while 68 percent of Indian people live in rural areas.[38] A PC costs Rs. 40,000—the equivalent of two years of average annual wages. Internet operation also requires basic literacy, and in a country where more than 40 percent of the population cannot read, an enormous swath of the country will not benefit from the technology. Even if the

"Internet culture" were to be embraced readily by Indian society, it would still have to deal with the issues of cyber crimes, for which the Indian government, especially the law enforcement agencies and the legislatures, is ill-prepared. Lastly, Internet-based transactions require credit card payment systems, which few Indians have access to.

Net Assessment: What Are the Prospects for an Internet/IT-Dependent Strategy?

None of this is to suggest that the Indian government should ignore the IT sector altogether. Bangalore is a success story, and it is true that the Internet has played a central role in the growth of the software industry and in the overall growth of the Indian economy.[39] But there are clearly limits to what can be achieved in high-technology industries operating in a developing nation. The emphasis (in high technology) could also exacerbate existing social cleavages: The benefactors of the Internet revolution will be the elite of the Indian population (dwelling in cities) engaged in the IT business. In the meantime, the chasm between the "haves" and "have nots" could widen, fueling class conflicts that have already reached a dangerous and perhaps irreversible juncture in India. Unless the Indian government can expand the Internet infrastructure laterally through comprehensive and sustained programs, a strategy of Internet-driven modernization will surely fail.

The assumption that the type of phenomenal growth as seen in Bangalore can be replicated in other parts of the country is also flawed. Favorable government policies and initiatives alone, given the paucity of material resources, infrastructure, and know-how in most parts of India, are insufficient to create "investor friendly" conditions. Instead, a conventional development model is required, one that seeks to develop an egalitarian society with a high literacy rate and unique social, economic, political, and infrastructure foundations.

At the same time, the opportunities the Internet provides—such as access to global markets, information, and education—as well as its inherent potential to accelerate development should be exploited.[40] The Internet, after all, is only a tool and cannot replace traditional models for development, especially in a developing country like India. Given the harsh reality of India's demography and existing disparities between urban and rural areas, heavy reliance on an Internet-driven modernization would be premature. Moreover, the arguments Michael Porter makes in a recent *Harvard Business Review* article provide a more realistic model of how the Internet can be incorporated into a company's (or country's) development strategy. He writes, "Many have argued that the Internet renders strategy obsolete. In reality, the opposite is true. Because the Internet tends to weaken industry profitability without providing propriety operational advantages, it is more important than ever for companies to distinguish themselves through strategy. The winners will be those that view Internet as a component to, not a cannibal of, traditional ways of competing."[41] This could not be more true for India, and the lesson is clear: The growth of the information technology industry, globally as well as in India, demands more, not less attention to the creation of a traditional development model for the country.

Notes

1. For investigative reports about corruption at the highest level in India see Aniruddha Bahal and Mathew Samuel, "Operation West End," May 14, 2001, http://www.tehelka.com/investigation/investigation1.htm.

2. The World Bank Group, "India at a Glance," World Development Indicators: Country Data, May 17, 2001, http://www.worldbank.org/cgi-bin/sendoff.cgi?page=%2Fdata%2Fcountrydata%2Faag%2Find_aag.pdf.

3. The World Bank Group, "India Country Brief 2000," September 15, 2000, http://lnweb18.worldbank.org/sar/sa.nsf/a22044d0c4877a3e852567de0052e0fa/bda6b892e28b548b852567ef005a0a85?OpenDocument.

4. The World Bank Group, "India Data Profile," World Development Indicators, July 2, 2000, http://www.worldbank.org/html/schools/regions/sasia/india.htm.

5. Jane's Information Group, "India Country Report," South Asia Intelligence Report, September 2000, www.janes.comYsentinel/south_asia/india.shtml.

6. Gary K. Bertch, Seema Gahlaut, and Anupam Srivastava, Engaging India: US Strategic Relations with the World's Largest Democracy (London: Routledge, 1999).

7. R. B. Heeks, India's Software Industry (New Delhi: Sage Publications, 1996).

8. Varun Sahni, "India as a Global Power: Capacity, Opportunity and Strategy," in Indian Foreign Policy: Agenda for the 21st Century, ed. Lalit Man Singh (New Delhi: Foreign Service Institute and Konark Publishers, 1997).

9. The terms "Internet" and "information technology" (IT) have been used simultaneously in this chapter because the Indian government does not make distinctions in many of its policies referring to the Internet. It instead broadly uses the term "IT," which includes the Internet among other related technologies.

10. The Internet/IT-related policies and initiatives taken by the government examined in the subsequent sections clarify India's intention to use the Internet/IT as the driver of India's development strategy.

11. A "traditional model of development" for the purpose of this chapter is described as a national development plan that seeks to develop fundamental infrastructures such as drinking water, public health, education, public security, public utilities, and key governance functions.

12. U.S. Department of State, "1998 Country Report on Economic Policy and Trade Practices: India," January 20, 2000, http://www.state.gov/www/issues/economic/trade_reports/south_asia98/india98.html.
13. Surendra K. Kaushik, "India's Evolving Economic Model: A Perspective on Economic and Financial Reforms," *The American Journal of Economics and Sociology* 56 (January 1, 1997), accessed November 19, 2001, http://web5.infotrac.galegroup.com/itw/infomark/258/506/17316704w5/purl=rc2_EA.
14. Ibid.
15. Estart.com, "India Country Profile," March 18, 2001, Indiawww.estart.com/india/news/fdishoot.
16. Kaushik, "India's Evolving Economic Model."
17. National Association of Software and Service Companies (NASSCOM), "Indian IT Industry," March 7, 2001, http://www.nasscom.org/template/inetec.htm.
18. Government of Karnataka, "About Bangalore," *Bangalore IT,* January 2, 2002, http://www.bangaloreit.com/html/aboutbng/history.htm.
19. Ibid.
20. Ambika Patni, "Silicon Valley of the East," *Harvard International Review,* 21, no. 4 (fall 1999): 8,9.
21. Mark Landler, "Hi I'm in Bangalore (But I Can't Say So)," *New York Times,* 21 March 2001.
22. Government of Karnataka, "About Bangalore."
23. Government of India, Planning Commission, "Ninth Five Year Plan 1997–2002," Information Technology, March 21, 2001, http://www.nic.in/ninthplan/vol2/v2c7–5htm.
24. Government of India, "IT for all by 2008," National Taskforce on Information Technology and Software Development, May 22, 1998, accessed March 21, 2001, http://it-taskforce.nic.in/vsit-taskforce/it2008.htm.
25. The case study of Bangalore is examined in detail in the next section of the chapter.
26. Madanmohan Rao, "India's IT Bill Follows the UNCITRAL's Model Law on E-Commerce," The Internet Society: On the Internet, March 23, 2001, http://www.isoc.org/oti/articles/0200/rao.html.
27. Government of Karnataka, "Karnataka—The Millennium IT Policy for the Common Man," CIO Space, March 20, 2001, wysiwyg://communities.itYty/ciospace/Itpolicy.asp. Also see http://www.virtualbangalore.com/business/kum/industry.htm.
28. Government of Karnataka, "New Industrial Policy and Package of Incentives and Concessions 1996–2001," G.O. No. CI/30/SPC/96: Bangalore, March 15, 2001, http://www.virtualbangalore.com/business/kum/industry.htm.
29. Government of India, "The Research and Development Cess Act, 1986 (As amended up to December 18, 1995)," March 23, 2001, http://www.nic.in/tdb/IOTA1.htm. Also see Government of India, "Technology Development Board," March 24, 2001, http://www.nic.in/Tdb/guid99.htm.
30. Ibid.
31. Government of India, Planning Commission, Ninth Five-Year Plan, 1997–2002.
32. VirtualBangalore.com, "Education," March 25, 2000, http://www.virtualbangalore.com/Edu/index.php3.
33. A "dhaba" is a traditional roadside Indian restaurant equipped with mud ovens. In its time the dhaba was a most desirable business venture, as is the dot-com today.
34. Charles Swett, "Strategic Assessment: The Internet," Office of the Assistant Secretary of Defense for Special Operations and Low-Intensity Conflict (Policy Planning), March 25, 2001, http://www.interesting-people.org/archive/2801.html.

35. Nassom, "India Internet Penetration Statistics," February 27, 2000, http://www.nasscom.org/template/inetec.htm.
36. Ibid.
37. The World Bank Group, "India Country Brief 2000."
38. Ibid.
39. NASSCOM, "Indian IT Industry."
40. "India: The Global Trade Management Solutions Market," *The Hindu*, March 6, 2001.
41. Michael E. Porter, "Strategy and the Internet," *Harvard Business Review* 79, no. 3 (spring 2001): 63.

CHAPTER 11

Brain Drain:
An Unintended Consequence of
Wiring Brazil?

Ryan McMichael[1]

Educating a populace to excel in the digital world is essential if a country is to prosper in the era of globalization. However, wiring the country also creates the possibility for a "brain drain," the emigration of a state's newly trained, technically skilled indigenous workers in search of a more prosperous future in another country. At first glance, Brazil would seem to be fertile ground for this phenomenon: Its economy and infrastructure dominate Latin America, but a large portion of the population still lives in poverty. Public and private entities are working assiduously to wire the population in an effort to improve the average standard of living, and in doing so may be increasing the possibility of brain drain.

Upon closer examination, though, high-tech worker emigration does not appear to be a problem in Brazil. While some Brazilians are moving to the United States for better employment opportunities, the trend is not as strong as one might expect. Instead, the same technical infrastructure built to educate Brazilians for globalization seems to be allowing them to employ their state-of-the-art skills worldwide without permanently leaving their native country. While brain drain is a major problem for some countries, Brazil provides an example of a nation concurrently developing an indigenous modern labor pool and the infrastructure to support its virtual employment worldwide.

Why Brazil?

Covering an area slightly smaller than the United States and with over 172 million citizens, Brazil is the largest and most populous country in South America.[2] With a gross domestic product (GDP) of over $1 trillion (1999 est.) and "possessing large and well developed agricultural, mining, manufacturing, and services sectors, Brazil's economy outweighs that of all other South American countries and is expanding its presence in world markets."[3] Brazil has been called the "poster child for the new global economy: a decentralized, dynamic, multidirectional marketplace in which anyone can play. With the eighth-largest economy in the world, . . . Brazil manufactures such sophisticated products as automobiles, airplanes and computers."[4]

Investors have taken note of this economic strength. Current U.S. private investments in Brazil total nearly $24 billion, followed closely by $20.4 billion from Spain.[5] The next three largest foreign investors are Holland ($8.8 billion), France ($7.8 billion), and Portugal ($7 billion).

Despite these strong overall figures, there remains a great disparity of individual income across the population. Like many countries, the Brazilian government has integrated into its effort to close this gap programs to disperse knowledge and high-tech skills through widespread Internet access. Currently, Internet use is growing faster in Latin America than in any other region in the world.[6] Brazil's 14.5 million Internet users represent a 67 percent increase since 1999, and 33 million more are expected to be online by 2003.[7] The Euromarketing Associates Institute predicts that by the end of 2001, Portuguese (Brazil's official language) will be the fastest growing language on the Internet.[8]

Going online is one thing, but as countless dot-com companies discovered in 2001, making money through the Internet is quite another. Many Brazilian companies seem to understand this: The country currently accounts for 90 percent of Latin American e-commerce.[9] Brazil receives 64 percent of all online advertising spending in Latin America, but more traditional retailers drive most Brazilian electronic commerce.[10] While online commerce totaled $2.47 billion in 2000, it was expected to reach nearly $40 billion by 2003 before the recent decline of technology firms in the United States.[11]

Its size and level of global integration make the Brazilian economy an important part of overall world financial markets. If an emerging brain drain becomes detrimental to Brazilian economic modernization, the effects will be felt far beyond the country's borders.

Current Efforts to Connect the People

The explosion in the number of Brazilians connecting to the Internet has not happened spontaneously. Numerous governmental, nongovernmental, and private organizations are working independently and in concert to connect all strata of the population to the Internet. The current online population of nearly 15 million people is remarkable considering the government first granted commercial Internet accesses in May of 1995.[12] The depth and the magnitude of these investments are rapidly creating a sizable labor pool with technical skills that are highly marketable around the globe.

Government Efforts

While the government is supporting several private and NGO education efforts, it is also working independently to reduce the cost of Internet access and equipment. Because of telecommunications deregulation (expected to be complete in 2002) and support for free-market competition, the cost of unlimited Internet access in Brazil averages $18 a month, compared to twice that amount in Mexico.[13] A law passed by the Brazilian Congress in January 2001 gives computer hardware, software, and cell phone manufacturers a 95 percent discount on industrialized products taxes. The law also requires these companies to give 5 percent of their profits to public universities, further increasing the investment in public education.[14] For millions of citizens, cheaper computers will mean Internet access from home instead of from their public school, work, or local civic center.

While tax relief and low service costs will benefit many middle-class families, regular personal computers will remain out of financial reach for many poor citizens. In an effort to break this cost barrier, the government created a project to develop a "Popular PC" (PPC) that costs around $300, or $15 a month for 24 months if financed through the state bank.[15] With government funding, researchers at the Federal

University of Minas Gerais built a prototype system with a 500 MHz-equivalent processor, 64 MB of RAM, an Ethernet network card, a 56K modem, 14-inch monitor, sound and video cards, serial and USB ports, a mouse and a keyboard.[16] To keep cost down the computer uses a Linux-based operating system instead of Microsoft Windows and a 16-MB flash memory card instead of a hard drive. According to the administrative committee for the Internet in Brazil, the main role of the PPC is Internet access, but consumers can use either virtual storage services or purchase inexpensive hard drives if they wish to store information. The government plans to provide the first production PPCs to schools, libraries, health posts, and communities to democratize Internet access, and then offer PPCs for sale to the general public.

Brazil has also teamed with several other countries to improve its technical education capabilities. On October 14, 1997, President Clinton and President Cardoso "launched an historic education partnership to advance their shared commitment to ensure that all our citizens have the tools they need to prosper in the 21st century economy."[17] The "U.S. Brazil Partnership: Improving Education in the 21st Century" Memorandum of Understanding (MOU) outlined four core areas of cooperation between the two countries, the first of which was "making sure that no child is left behind in the Information Revolution." To accomplish this goal, both countries agreed to support a broad range of initiatives:

1. Public-Private Sector Dialogue on Technology in the Classroom—Encourage and direct private sector support to provide access to technology and increase the ability of students in both countries to use tools to learn in the new global economy.
2. Providing Access to Education Technology in Rural Communities—Increase access to education and information technologies for the thousands of rural communities, which currently are without electricity, in partnership with the Clean Energy Agreement and Brazil's PRODEEM program.
3. Next Generation Internet—Collaborate in the development of the Next Generation Internet Initiative to increase the technological capabilities of both countries' educational systems.
4. Linking Classrooms in the United States and Brazil—Collaborate to increase high-tech computer link-ups between classrooms, teachers, and students in the U.S. and Brazil.[18]

As a part of a related agreement, the International Data Group of Brazil, working with the Brazilian information technology community, agreed to launch a TechCorps Brazil chapter, modeled on the U.S. TechCorps initiative. TechCorps Brazil would place volunteers from the technology community in Brazilian schools as advisors and mentors assisting introduction and integration of new technologies.[19] The original MOU ran for two years; in October 1999, Brazil's education minister and the U.S. Department of Education secretary agreed to extend the agreement through the end of 2002.[20] The officials also agreed to expand the scope of the program to include additional teacher exchanges and Internet links among schools and teachers in both countries.

Brazil is also working with Venezuela and Colombia to develop math and science educational software over the Internet. Known as the International Virtual Education Network (IVEN), the program links teams of educators from each country to "develop software that emphasizes learn-by-doing and simulation that covers the entire math and science curriculum at the secondary level, including math, biology, chemistry, and physics."[21] The goal of IVEN is to reduce the cost of implementing technology-based education tools into the public class-room. Each country has teams consisting of a master teacher, a graphic artist, a content specialist, an instructional designer, and a software developer.[22] As each team develops a curricular unit, known as a module, they will add the design to their online page for other teams to evaluate. Once the lesson designs are accepted, they will be viewable on IVEN with a browser. Schools without Internet access will be able to order the modules on CD-ROM.

Private Efforts

All of these government efforts show great promise in bringing the Internet to schools and to semiskilled workers with some disposable income, but what about the working poor and those living in Brazil's city slums? Fortunately the government is not the only group helping disseminate technology to the masses. There are many examples of private citizens working to bridge the digital divide in Brazil. One of the most successful has been Rodrigo Baggio, founder and president of the Committee for Computer Science Democratization (CDI; www.cdi. org.br). In November 2000, CNN en Espanol named Baggio one of the "Twenty Latin American Leaders of the Internet."[23]

Working as a high school teacher in the early 1990s, Baggio launched an effort to convince businesses to donate computers to poor communities so citizens could learn the skills necessary for escaping the *favelas* (slums) of Rio de Janeiro. In 1994, he quit his high school teaching job to open the first Community Computer

School in Rio. On its opening day, the school received extensive media coverage and soon volunteers and donors flocked to provide equipment and services. Six years later, CDI has opened 116 additional computer schools in 13 Brazilian states and has graduated more than 35,000 students from its intensive three-month program.[24] Many graduates have found jobs that employ their newfound computer skills, while others have become teachers in the schools from which they graduated.

Students pay $10 per month for instruction that includes word processing, accounting programs, spreadsheets, and computer graphics.[25] The fee covers the salaries of each school's teachers, which at $200 a month is nearly twice that of a public school teacher. CDI employs 16 full-time staffers, but the organization is really held together by the 140-plus volunteers who donate their time and expertise and numerous sponsors, including Microsoft, Ashoka, Global Partners, and the United Methodist Church, who donate equipment and funds to the schools. CDI is but one of many private initiatives to bridge the digital divide in Brazil, but its highly successful approach has captured the attention of many, including President Clinton, who visited one of the schools in 1997.[26] Recently, CDI has helped establish similar but autonomous programs in Colombia, Uruguay, and Mexico.

Combined Efforts

While CDI has proven successful in training many *favelas* residents in basic computer skills, the three-month course by no means prepares students for an IT-specific career. Recognizing this, CDI has teamed with Rio Online and Viva Rio to form Rio Digital. Rio Online is a governmental organization started in 1997 by the municipal government of Rio de Janeiro and private-sector partners to develop a program similar to CDI. Viva Rio is a nongovernmental organization formed in 1993 "which has focused on creating projects to improve the living situation of the people of Rio de Janeiro over the long term. Currently, Viva runs more than 25 projects in the areas of education, community development, human rights, and public safety."[27] Rio Digital plans to open 12 "pilot" centers with services that better meet the growing demand for special IT training.

The goal of the program is to "raise the number of small businesses, create new job opportunities and employment prospects and raise incomes."[28] Rio Digital hopes to provide training and computer access to "micro-entrepreneurs, youth, and the unemployed, with special emphasis on developing entrepreneurship." The goal is to create business owners instead of office workers. Total project costs are estimated to be $1.446 million. The Inter-American Development Bank (IABD) is funding 60 percent of the program ($860,000) with Rio Digital and Cisco Systems providing the additional funds ($382,000 and $204,000, respectively).[29]

These represent only a few of the many community, state, national, and international efforts to bring Internet access and technical skills to the average Brazilian citizen. While these groups are supporting the ultimate goal of a more affluent and economically secure populace, there is perhaps a negative consequence for Brazil.

Will the New Skilled Workers Leave?

After developing the skills necessary to compete in a globalized economy, many technical workers have the ability to offer their services to the global free market. One unintended consequence of increased Internet access, the Popular PC, the U.S.-Brazil partnership, IVEN, and Rio Digital may be that the talented workers leave their home country and take their skills and entrepreneurial ideas with them. While the financial benefits for such an individual are potentially enormous, Brazilian society as a whole will not receive a return on its investment. If such a trend were to emerge, Brazil could become an unfortunate case study of the unintended consequences of high-technology training and education programs.

While opportunities exist around the world, many high-tech workers who choose to leave home are drawn to the United States, the center of the technology development world. While demand for technical workers in the United States is cyclical, top talent is always in demand. A CDI instructor who makes $200 a month teaching Brazilian students could easily make more than that each day as a software instructor for a consulting firm. Even for a minimum-wage position, a full-time worker will make more than this each week. For some, the prospect of such an income is enough to lead them to seek employment in the United States. Once this decision is made, a person has two primary options for gaining U.S. employment: apply for a temporary visa for specialty occupation workers, or apply for permanent residency.

The temporary visa program, known as the H-1B program, has received a great deal of public attention over the past few years. Responding to pressure from U.S. industry, Congress passed the American Competitiveness and Workforce Improvement Act of 1998

(ACWIA). The ACWIA increased the number of H-1B visas that could be issued from 65,000 in fiscal year 1998 to 115,000 in fiscal years 1999 and 2000, and 107,5000 in fiscal year 2001. In 2002, the number of visas would return to 65,000. This temporary increase was intended to help fill the shortage of technology workers available in the United States. H-1B visas are good for six years, after which an employer must reapply for another visa or the worker must return to their native country.

Figure 11.1 shows the number of nonimmigrants admitted from Brazil as temporary workers on H1 visas for the years 1991 to 1998 (data not available for 1997). Before 1996, the INS did not separate H-1A workers (registered nurses) from H-1B workers (workers with specialty occupations). Furthermore, of the H-1B visas, only a portion was for high-technology positions. According to the U.S. labor department on H-1 positions, in fiscal year 1996, "41.5 percent were computer-related occupations—which are considered high-tech workers—19.5 percent were for therapists, 4.9 percent were for other medical and health professionals, and 2.9 percent were for college university faculty, 2.5 percent for registered nurses, 2.4 percent for accountant auditors, and 2.3 percent for physicians."[30] Therefore, based on these percentages, of the 3,369 Brazilians approved for H-1B visas in fiscal year 1998, approximately 1,400 were for computer-related positions, slightly less than 120 per month.

As the demand for technology workers grew, the H-1B distribution adjusted accordingly. By the first half of fiscal year 2000, INS reported that the percentage of H-1B visas for computer-related occupations increased to nearly 54 percent.[31] While 1999 and 2000 statistical data is not currently publicly available, this same INS report, "Characteristics of Special Occupation Workers (H-1B): October 1999 to February 2000," indicated that during this five-month period 861 petitions from Brazil were approved. Applying the new percentage, just over 161 workers per month would be entering the computer profession. This represents a 34.5 percent increase in the number of Brazilians with high-tech skills temporarily moving to the United States. But were they staying?

The numbers suggest they are not. While the number of Brazilian immigrants seeking temporary employment in the United States technology industry was growing throughout the 1990s, the total number of immigrants seeking permanent residency was relatively constant (Figure 11.2).[32] Moreover, the number of professional and technical immigrants that decided to permanently relocate to the United States (Figure 11.3) actually decreased toward the end of the decade, dropping

Figure 11.1[33]

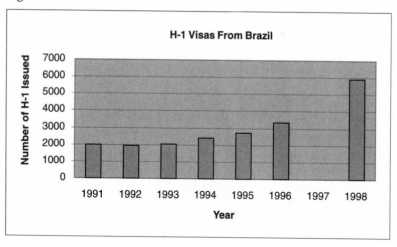

nearly 50 percent from 1996 to 1998. This is in sharp contrast to the trend in temporary workers.

So Far, No Brain Drain

Based on these numbers, there is an apparent trend of Brazilian high-tech workers moving temporarily to the United States, but far fewer seem to be relocating permanently—in other words, there appears to be no brain drain, at least in the Brazilian case. The emigration of a state's technically skilled indigenous workers in search of a more prosperous future in another country is surely less of a threat if the workers intend to return to their native country after a certain period of time. A Brazilian spending five or six years in the United States under the H-1B program might pay taxes in the United States instead of Brazil during that period, and in other ways detract from the Brazilian economy. But if they do return, such workers will bring knowledge and professional relationships that will be worth far more in the long run. It amounts to about the same period of time, for example, that many Brazilian students spend in the United States completing advanced degrees at American universities.

A better way to understand the brain drain threat, therefore, would be to rephrase the definition to speak of the *permanent* emigration of a state's technically skilled indigenous workers in search of a more

Figure 11.2[34]

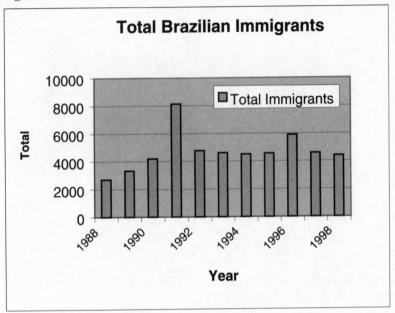

prosperous future in another country. Even with this new meaning, the numbers tell only part of the story—and few numbers exist to describe the intentions or state of mind of temporarily resident Brazilians.

To fill this information gap in an initial, anecdotal way, I conducted a highly informal, subjective survey of Brazilian students currently studying at three top American universities: Harvard, the Massachusetts Institute of Technology, and Stanford. I e-mailed these students under the assurance of nonattribution. While they acknowledged the appeal of working in the United States, the desire to return to Brazil was fervent. Many pointed out that, by building a strong Internet infrastructure, the country actually allowed them to have the best of both worlds: They can continue working for American or other high-tech companies and demand the same salaries they would have in Palo Alto, but reside in Brazil with their friends and families, at a much lower cost of living and with what they view as a significantly higher quality of life.

Temporary H-1B workers are permitted to return to their home countries and maintain employment with the companies they worked with in the United States. In fact, many U.S. companies have argued that

Figure 11.3[35]

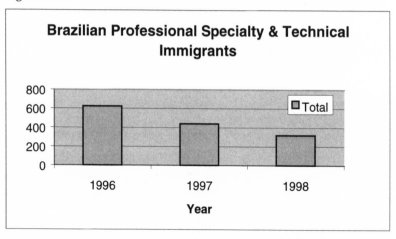

this is specifically why they need H-1B workers: In Congressional hearings on the H-1B issue, Austin Fragomen of the American Council of International Personnel testified that many companies hire workers under the H-1B program to teach them the company's corporate culture before sending them to run an office or division in their native country.[36] Additionally, as private investment by foreign companies in Brazil continues to grow, the demand for high-tech workers in the country increases as well. Just as in the United States, demand is outpacing the available supply of skilled workers. A Brazilian student studying in Boston described it this way: "Many companies in Brazil were hiring top executives in the U.S. I can account that from my own experience, for I know many recent graduates (MBAs, PhDs and undergrads) that are going back to Brazil this semester, not only because they like Brazil but because they got better offers from Brazilian companies."[37]

If a high-tech worker can perform the same work with the same pay from his home country, the job itself will rarely be the motivating factor when deciding weather or not to relocate to another country. Some souls are inherently nomadic, but based on correspondence with these students the argument for increased brain drain due to improved technical education and experience has little weight in Brazil. And of course, for many it's not only about the money; one student wrote that, "At least among all the Brazilians students I know, most of them would like to do something to improve Brazil, which reinforces the idea of returning home."[38]

And while many support the current government efforts, there is also a belief that officials are not doing enough to promote the IT sector. "The role of the government should be in fostering human capital but also using it," one student wrote. "There are many different efforts in Brazil to prepare people for the new economy, but I would not say that they are really doing anything. I am probably being too hard, for there are several programs in Brazil looking to do that. What I know for a fact is that the debate is only beginning in Brazil so it will be interesting to see what happens."[39]

What is especially striking about many of these students is how passionate they are about improving their country. Responses were filled with phrases expressing devotion to their homeland and their sense of duty to improve the economic standing of their fellow citizens. Many have realized that education is only part of the solution and are working to teach the importance of developing a strong technical infrastructure that Brazilians can use. One put it this way: "I am writing about the importance of investment in human capital and that we must have a well educated work force for the future. Whether they will leave the country or remain in Brazil will depend on what is the situation in Brazil. I believe people leave their country when there are no opportunities. However, this can be changed."[40]

There is strong reason to believe, therefore, that the brain drain phenomenon need not be a problem for Brazil. However, if Brazil cannot continue to expand and maintain the country's technical infrastructure, more high-tech workers will feel compelled to emigrate to remain in their chosen profession. Furthermore, if Brazil suffers another economic crisis like it had in the early 1990s, all bets are off—though much the same could be said for any country with a well-educated but underutilized work force.

Still a Substantial Promise

Neither the number of Brazilians with high-tech skills immigrating to the United States nor the brief survey of Brazilian students studying in America indicates that brain drain is currently a problem for Brazil. Despite the substantial public and private investment in high-technology infrastructure and the resulting increase in the number of citizens with skills that are in high demand around the world, the number of Brazilians deciding to permanently relocate to the United States for employment is actually decreasing. The Brazilian students who contributed to this effort want to learn as much as they can while abroad, but they do intend to return home, as one student wrote: "Most people I know are planning to go back to Brazil. I personally will go back. It does not mean that I will have to go right away; I will take advantage of all the opportunities I have in the U.S., so that I can better myself, and then head home."[41]

Of course, the whole idea of brain drain is of little public interest as of late. Since the "correction" to the inflated NASDAQ, the demand for high-tech workers has decreased significantly. In contrast to news stories with headlines like "Forget the Huddled Masses: Send Nerds"[42] from 1998, recent headlines such as "Sad Plight of Fired H-1B Workers"[43] reflect the dramatic decline in demand for foreign technology employees. When numerous H-1B visa holders are losing their jobs and returning to their native countries, the idea of brain drain being a significant risk to a rapidly developing economy holds little sway. However, as globalization and increasing economic integration continue, the fear that a developing economy will lose the best and brightest workers will periodically generate debate. The experience of Brazil suggests that these counterproductive results can be avoided.

Notes

1. The author is employed as an engineer for Photon Research Associates, Inc., of San Diego, CA. The opinions and conclusions expressed in this paper are exclusively those of the author and do not represent those of PRA or any of its customers.
2. U.S. Central Intelligence Agency, *The World Factbook 2000*, http://www.cia.gov/cia/publications/factbook/geos/br.html.
3. Ibid.
4. Patrick Symmes, "Agressivo," *Wired Archive*, October 1997, http://www.wired.com/wired/archive/5.10/travel_brazil_pr.html.
5. Paulo Rebelo, "Spanish Pesetas Flow Into Brazil," *Wired News*, January 9, 2001, http://www.wired.com/news/print/0,1294,40889,00.html.
6. Inter-American Development Bank, "Internet Must Help Latin America Achieve Its Social Goals," March 19, 2001, http://www.iadb.org/exr/PRENSA/2001/cp5901e.htm.
7. Paulo Rebelo, "Brazil ISPs Drop Like Dot-Coms," *Wired News*, February 9, 2001, http://www.wired.com/news/business/0,1367,41652,00.html.
8. "Information Technology Program 'Rio Digital,'" Project Number TC-01-01-06-4-BR, Inter-American Development Bank, January 26, 2001, http://www.iadb.org/exr/doc98/pro/pbr1064.pdf.
9. Ibid.
10. Julia Scheeres, "Brazil's Amazonian Net Reach," *Wired News*, February 1, 2001, http://www.wired.com/news/business/0,1367,41562,00.html.

11. Ibid.
12. Maria Ercilla, "Market Forces: Brazil, Not the Movie," *Hotwired,* June 1996, http://hotwired.lycos.com/market/96/21/brazil.html.
13. Scheeres, "Brazil's Amazonian Net Reach."
14. Paulo Rebelo, "Brazil May Slash Computer Taxes," *Wired News,* January 9, 2001, http://www.wired.com/news/politics/0,1283,41060,00.html.
15. Paulo Rebelo, "Brazil Counting On Net Gain," *Wired News,* February 23, 2001, http://www.wired.com/news/print/0,1294,41785,00.html.
16. Ibid.
17. U.S. Embassy Brazil, "Memorandum of Understanding on Education between the Government of the United States of America and the Government of the Federative Republic of Brazil," October 14, 1997, www.embaixadaamericana.org.br/index.php?amp;action=materia&id=450&submenu=5&itemmenu=70.
18. Ibid.
19. Ibid.
20. U.S. Embassy Brazil, "U.S. and Brazil Strengthen Partnership for Education," January 11, 2001, www.embaixadaamericana.org.br/index.php?action=materia&id=447&submenu=5&itemmenu=70.
21. Katie Dean, "Knowledge Knows No Boundaries," *Wired News,* April 19, 2001, http://www.wired.com/news/culture/0,1284,42660,00.html.
22. Ibid.
23. AOL Time Warner, "Twenty Latin American Leaders of the Internet Named by CNN en Espanol," November 16, 2000, http://media.aoltimewarner.com/media/cb_press_view.cfm?release_num=50251794.
24. Daniela Hart, "Combating Technological Apartheid in Brazilian *Favelas,*" *Changemakers.net,* May 2000, http://www.changemakers.net/journal/00may/hart.cfm.
25. Ashoka Fellow Profile, "Rodrigo Baggio," May 2000, http://www.ashoka.org/viewprofile1.cfm?PersonId=1199.
26. Keith Suter, "Rodrigo Baggio's Computer Literacy Program For Brazil's Disadvantaged," *Radio 2GB News Commentary,* August 4, 2000, http://www.wesleymission.org.au/ministry/suter/4aug00.htm.
27. "Information Technology Program 'Rio Digital.'"
28. Ibid.
29. Ibid.
30. U.S. Immigration and Naturalization Service, *1996 Statistical Yearbook of the Immigration and Naturalization Service* (Washington, DC: U.S. Government Printing Office, October 1997), "Table 40. Non-immigrants Admitted as Temporary Workers, Exchange Visitors, and Intra-Company Transferees by Region and Selected Country of Citizenship."
31. U.S. Immigration and Naturalization Service, "Characteristics of Specialty Occupation Workers (H-1B): October 1999 to February 2000," (Washington, DC: U.S. Government Printing Office, June 2000).
32. The peak in 1992 is probably associated with economic refugees fleeing the inflationary troubles occurring in Brazil at the time.
33. U.S. Immigration and Naturalization Service, *Statistical Yearbook of the Immigration and Naturalization Service,* 1991 to 1998 (Washington, DC: U.S. Government Printing Office, 1991: September 1992; 1992: October 1993; 1993: September 1994; 1994: February 1996; 1995: March 1997; 1996: October 1997; 1998: November 2000), "Table 40. Non-immigrants Admitted as Temporary Workers,

Exchange Visitors, and Intra-Company Transferees by Region and Selected Country of Citizenship."

34. U.S. Immigration and Naturalization Service, *1998 Statistical Yearbook of the Immigration and Naturalization Service* (Washington, DC: U.S. Government Printing Office, November 2000), "Table 10. Immigrants Admitted by Region and Country of Birth Fiscal Years 1988–98."

35. U.S. Immigration and Naturalization Service, *Statistical Yearbook of the Immigration and Naturalization Service,* 1996 to 1998 (Washington, DC: U.S. Government Printing Office, 1996: October 1997; 1997: October 1999; 1998: November 2000), "Table 21. Immigrants Admitted by Major Occupation Group and Region and Selected Country of Birth."

36. Statement of Austin Fragomen, Chairman, American Council of International Personnel, "H-1B Temporary Professional Worker Visa Program and Information Technology Workforce Issues," Hearing before the Subcommittee on Immigration and Claims of the Committee on the Judiciary, House of Representatives, 106th Cong., August 5, 1999, serial no. 31.

37. E-mail from Brazilian student studying in the United States, April 14, 2001.

38. Ibid.

39. E-mail from Brazilian student studying in the United States, April 17, 2001.

40. Ibid.

41. Ibid.

42. *Business Week* headline, as referenced in U.S. General Accounting Office, "Information Technology: Assessment of the Department of Commerce's Report on Workforce Demand and Supply" (Washington, DC: U.S. Government Printing Office, March 1998).

43. Swaroopa Iyengar, "Sad Plight of Fired H-IB Workers," *Wired News,* March 13, 2001, http://www.wired.com/news/politics/0,1283,42369,00.html.

CHAPTER 12

www.AfricanOpportunity.com

Amanda Olson

President Clinton visited the African continent in February 2000 and remarked, "We must think of ourselves as children of one common world. If we wish to deepen peace and prosperity and democracy for ourselves, we must wish it also for the people of Africa. Africa is the cradle of humanity, but also a big part of humanity's future."[1] His high-profile tour of the struggling continent focused attention on both African successes and failures. Americans were confronted with the notion that the health of the African continent directly affects the United States due to significant security, economic, and cultural investments there.

U.S. policy in Africa must be reconciled with the economic and security initiatives it currently supports there, and the potential role of information technology must be examined in relation to U.S. aid and engagement programs. The efforts of the U.S. military and an Internet connection agenda called the Leland Initiative are powerful programs, but they could become more effective through greater coordination with regional organizations in Africa, such as the Economic Community of West African States (ECOWAS), to utilize existing relationships, efforts, and leaders. The three programs together can help the United

States attain its goals of promoting democracy, increasing security, improving education, and strengthening the economy.

U.S. Policy in Africa

The United States has directed increasing resources to Africa since the end of the cold war. The Clinton administration embraced African initiatives and President Clinton made a number of high profile tours of the continent. Through rhetoric and diplomatic speeches, policy implications were hinted: peace, justice, prosperity, and, most importantly, engagement. One of his speeches, in Nigeria, identified specific goals the United States has for Africa:

> Americans look upon Africa not simply as a continent with problems, but also as a continent which presents the world's next great opportunity to advance the cause of peace, justice, and prosperity . . . we are also committed to working . . . to help build stronger institutions, improve education, fight disease, crime and corruption, ease the burden of debt and promote trade and investment in a way that brings more of the benefits of prosperity to people who have embraced democracy.[2]

These are ambitious promises and goals, but President Clinton admitted that the United States cannot possibly solve Africa's problems. Africa needs to make a decision to implement change; America can only offer assistance. One challenge for Washington, then, is to determine specific means that are appropriate to reach such goals.

Already, the United States has been involved in multiple African conflicts in the 1990s that required security personnel and used budgets, supplies, and expertise from the security field. One example is the 1992 Operation Provide Relief, which was initiated to aid refugees fleeing the conflict and drought in Somalia. U.S. military aircraft, government-funded civilian craft, and ships delivered over 380,000 tons of relief supplies throughout the mission. Besides the enormous costs and resources involved, the highest price was the death of 44 American soldiers and the 175 injured during the mission.

When the United States finally withdrew from Somalia, the politically difficult circumstances resonated throughout the security community and directly affected future decisions regarding American involvement in peacekeeping and remote conflicts. Although the United States has expressed little traditional security interest in Africa,[3] Somalia demonstrates the noteworthy ways the United States can become embroiled on the continent regardless of that interest. If the United States is planning to be involved in further stabilization of Africa, a clear and effective policy is crucial. The U.S. Department of Defense has recognized its paradoxical role for Africa. Although there is a lack of traditional interest, the department plans to maintain a "leading role" in African issues through four policy goals that include: promoting peace, providing humanitarian assistance, fostering democracy and respect for human rights, and supporting economic growth and sustainable development.[4]

Organizations to Facilitate American Policy

U.S. goals for Africa mirror those of its broad foreign policy—peace, humanitarian works, democracy, human rights, and prosperity. The fact that these goals are difficult to attain does not mean that they should be discounted; there are relationships and assistance plans currently in place in Africa to facilitate the objectives. However, policy makers could augment progress with a more concentrated effort to bind programs together and achieve mutual goals. Integrating the programs would allow for synergy between resources, personnel, contacts, and regional expertise. The three initiatives undertaken by the Leland Initiative, ECOWAS, and United States European Command (USEUCOM) share ambitions of economic and political security, and they demonstrate the role information technology can play in twenty-first-century aid programs.

The Leland Initiative

The Leland Initiative is a U.S. government program intended to extend Internet capabilities to 20 or more African countries. The five-year program has a $15 million budget and targets four goals: improving connectivity in Africa, increasing access to information on sustainable development, enhancing the ability of Africans to find solutions to African problems, and making African-produced information available to the rest of the world.[5] The initiative is also intended to underwrite other U.S. policy goals, especially fostering democracy and supporting economic growth and sustainable development.[6] The Internet could offer investors in Africa the same opportunity it is already extending companies elsewhere: to develop outposts with global reach and advanced technology, even in an area with little infrastructure. A company that requires connectivity, but little else in the way of infrastructure, can infuse development into a country quickly and profitably. The

Leland Initiative aims to add the connections necessary to make Africa desirable to such companies.

To achieve the desired results, the Leland Initiative has three strategic objectives. First, it seeks to create an "enabling policy environment" with affordable prices, private-sector Internet Service Providers (ISPs), and free and open access to information available on the web. Second, the program aims to create a sustainable supply of Internet services with effective, indigenous ISPs, countrywide access with special attention to the rural areas, and society chapters serving as advocacy and support organizations. Finally, the Leland Initiative seeks to enhance Internet use for sustainable development through information-sharing partnerships, increased capacity for Africans to use information when making decisions and managing resources, and broader user bases for information systems along with indigenous training capacities.[7] Countries involved in the Leland Initiative include Benin, Botswana, Côte d'Ivoire, Eritrea, Ethiopia, Ghana, Guinea Bissau, Guinea, Kenya, Madagascar, Malawi, Mali, Mozambique, Namibia, Rwanda, Senegal, South Africa, Tanzania, Uganda, Zambia, and Zimbabwe.[8]

As Leland planners work within those countries to enhance economic development, the U.S. military is actively involved in Africa promoting security interests. A strong economy and a stable security situation have been linked throughout history. That suggests varied but complimentary goals in which societal stability and security and economic development advance in mutually supportive ways.

USEUCOM

United States European Command (USEUCOM) is tasked with handling African security relations. The commander's vision for the theater is "a community of free, stable, and prosperous nations acting in concert while respecting the dignity and rights of the individual and adhering to the principles of sovereignty and international law."[9] To achieve this, USEUCOM embraced the Quadrennial Defense Review's strategic concept of "Shape, Respond, and Prepare." To this end, USEUCOM has been involved in administering the African Crisis Response Initiative (ACRI) program as well as conducting medical exercises, regional exercises, programs to improve military professionalism, and civil affairs democracy seminars among other initiatives. Additionally, the command has specified particular interests in West Africa, including conflict prevention, democratization, health, population growth, the environment, and U.S. investments in mining, energy, and telecommunications.

USEUCOM coordinates the military aspects of the interagency effort ACRI. The ACRI is designed to train 12,000 troops from militaries selected from across the continent. The skills enable troops to respond quickly and effectively to peacekeeping and humanitarian conflicts. The program is compatible with U.S. policy, which indicates African countries should take primary responsibility for African affairs and thereby reduce the U.S. burden. ACRI has requested $20 million from the fiscal year (FY) 2001 peacekeeping account for training exercises, nonlethal basic equipment, and troops from Senegal, Uganda, Malawi, Mali, Ghana, Benin, and Côte d'Ivoire.[10] Secondary training has occurred in Ghana, Senegal, Mali, Benin, and Malawi. The training often includes computer-assisted training exercises that offer opportunities for military-to-military exchanges among officers from the African nations . That, in turn, enhances the exchange of information and standards and builds relationships simply through communication. At the moment, there is no evidence that USEUCOM possesses an ability to remain in contact with the officers or to keep them in touch with one another once training is complete. Security cannot be expected through a mere Internet connection, but perhaps a continued relationship would enhance the U.S.-led training and objectives if the military members could remain connected via the Internet after official training was finished.

Why ECOWAS?

The U.S. attempt to realize policy goals through Internet connections and military partnerships would be more effective if it took advantage of existing African regional organizations. Africa's individual countries cannot be treated as a single entity—but that is just what most U.S. policies and aid programs tend to do. An effort that focuses on some of the structure that Africans have attempted to create themselves could be a more effective way to produce change; the relationships and networks already exist and the African leaders have developed a forum for discussion.

ECOWAS is one such organization, and the United States should attempt to work within that structure for change. The relative prosperity and democracy enjoyed by West African states such as Côte d'Ivoire, Cape Verde, Ghana, and Nigeria provide a solid foundation on which to begin such an extensive effort. West Africa also has the successful role model of Senegal, which achieved full Internet connectivity in 1996 and created an explosion for itself of information technology–based services.[11] The United States may choose to include other regional forums, such as the South African Development Council (SADC) or the

East African Defense Commission (EADC). Choosing a regional focus does not mean one region should be excluded over another but only that solid organizations should be utilized and strengthened while promoting U.S. policy.

ECOWAS originated in 1975 as a regional group of states dedicated to economic growth. As stated on the official ECOWAS website, "The vision that the founding fathers had at the time of the creation of ECOWAS was one of collective self-sufficiency through the integration of the sixteen West African countries into an economic block with a single market organized around an economic and monetary union."[12] By suppressing duties, stabilizing taxes among the states, establishing a common tariff, harmonizing policies, and creating a monetary zone, ECOWAS intended to make the member states more competitive in an increasingly global world. Twenty-five years later, the organization can boast modest but real achievements: a freer movement of persons, construction of interstate roads, and the development of telecommunication links.

However, ECOWAS has encountered serious difficulties in its original goals as well. The liberalized, integrated market has not materialized, external tariffs are completely absent, and harmonized policies are in the early design phase.[13] The obvious failures stand in stark contrast to a surprising development in the ECOWAS agenda: In 1978, the Authority of Heads of State and Government adopted a nonaggression protocol. In 1981 a defense assistance protocol was implemented, and in 1991 ECOWAS issued a declaration of political principles.[14] These actions have resulted in an ECOWAS increasingly involved in regional peace and security including the conflicts in Liberia, Sierra Leone, and Guinea Bissau. The Economic Community of West African States Monitoring Group (ECOMOG), the security arm of ECOWAS, played a mediation and peacekeeping role during the Liberian civil war, reinstated the democratically elected government of Sierra Leone in 1998, and struggled to reinstate the government in Guinea Bissau. It is not merely an economic forum any longer.

Although the successes were followed by setbacks (Liberia and Sierra Leone have since re-erupted into conflict and the action in Guinea Bissau was not successful), ECOWAS has emerged as even more determined to stabilize the region. "Drawing lessons [from the events in Guinea Bissau] . . . the Executive Secretariat of ECOWAS initiated the establishment of a mechanism for the prevention, management and settlement of conflicts and for the maintenance of peace and security in the sub-region."[15] The organization shifted from a reactive attitude to a proactive force. They developed the Regional Observation and Monitoring Center, designed to give warning of an impending crisis. Information transmitted to the center is compiled and tracks any breakdowns or stress between member states. Four centers were created in Banjul (the Gambia), Cotonou (Benin), Monrovia (Liberia), and Ouagadougou (Burkina Faso). A mediation and security council makes emergency decisions during a crisis and the Defense and Security Commission may advise.[16] ECOWAS is becoming an energetic force relying on information, technology, and discussion to achieve a more stable West Africa.

Other entities have noted ECOWAS intentions and successes. The United States has requested $1 million from the peacekeeping operations account for FY2001 to enhance ECOWAS staff training, equipment maintenance, medical gear, and transportation support. Additionally, $2 million was requested to facilitate training and joint exercises among regional groups such as ECOWAS, SADC, and EADC.[17] "ECOWAS has been a key player in promoting regional stability and providing humanitarian response in West Africa."[18] A U.S. official reiterated the congressional justification: "The Economic Community of West African States (ECOWAS) is particularly interested in 'what we call security architecture or how to respond to crises like Liberia and Sierra Leone . . . we hope to work with them to develop peacekeeping structures that will allow them to take a regional political mandate and translate that into a military presence on the ground.'"[19] ECOWAS exemplifies what U.S. policy states it seeks: Africans desiring change and working to create it. ECOWAS's commitment to both security and economic success, as well as its experimentation with technology in order to achieve this, make its goals compatible with the Leland Initiative and USEUCOM efforts. The relevant question regarding technology-assisted development, then, is whether the Internet can help achieve ECOWAS and USEUCOM goals in any meaningful way.

Coordinating Efforts

ECOWAS appears to demonstrate that the West African community is interested in enhancing its own economic and security environment. The organization has a 25-year history and meets regularly to discuss issues and involvement plans. However, the conflicts in Sierra Leone, Liberia, and the failure in Guinea-Bissau also demonstrate that the organization is lacking in capability; the mandate and passion are there but the tools are not. Conversely, the United States has demonstrated interest in Africa and is actively engaged in the security situation there through USEUCOM. Washington also provides large amounts of economic assistance, including the massive $15 million Leland Initiative. The missing link is the combination of these three programs for a

truly powerful force in Western Africa. A concerted effort among
ECOWAS leaders and personnel, U.S. military, and Leland professionals would allow the United States to reach its goals while West Africa
became more secure and prosperous in the process. ECOWAS,
USEUCOM, and the Leland Initiative all have information, discussion,
and technology as elements in their plan. Rather than dispersing aid and
resources haphazardly, the U.S. initiatives should facilitate cooperation
among the leaders of all three organizations—and, although its role will
be supportive rather than central, a stronger Internet connection in
West Africa could help make these goals a reality.

The Power of Connections

Promoting Democracy

An idea commonly suggested in discussions on Internet and globalization is that the Internet enhances the growth and maintenance of
democracy. Democracy requires free information flows and access to
alternative viewpoints, and the Internet provides that. Information
flows in Ghana were attributed recently with promoting political
discussion and changing the outcomes of an election.[20] In this case, the
medium was FM radio, but the result was that information translated
into democratic principles. Before the elections, citizens were demanding an end to corruption and unemployment. The Minister of Justice in
the new government remarked, "The minute people were able to talk
freely—and anonymously—on the radio, and ask what officials were
up to, was the beginning of accountability for government in Ghana."[21]
The FM stations allowed participation by the citizens and publication
of fraudulent election practices. "Ghanaians going to the polls would
call their local FM station if they saw any shenanigans, and it would be
broadcast in seconds. The radios were monitored by the election and it
would quickly respond."[22] Thomas Friedman adds that the four most
democratic countries in West Africa all have private radio stations. "So
let's stop sending Africa lectures on democracy," Friedman writes.
"Let's instead make all aid, all I.M.F.- World Bank loans, all debt relief
conditional on African governments' permitting free FM radio stations.
Africans will do the rest."[23]

Friedman's statement addresses the participation and accountability
challenges to democratic development in Africa. Although the radio
allows participation by even the illiterate and those who cannot afford

luxury items like computers, the Internet can also play an important role in any democracy-building plan in Africa. The Internet functions as a valuable research tool to those who are literate, and they, in turn, can spread information to the illiterate or unconnected. The research capabilities separate the Internet from past information technologies and make it a crucial adjunct to traditional democracy-building tools in the developing world.

Even in Africa, there are already powerful examples of the Internet's potential. Nigeria experienced the power of the Internet as a research tool when journalists discovered the extent of corruption in their government via web publications.[24] In Ghana, journalists also rely on the web for research. One journalist remarked that the web allowed him to access the same information that those in more developed countries were able to find. "You can easily access and search for background information in a way we never could before. I can check on companies that are investing here."[25] Powerful research connections promote powerful journalism and that translates into an informed citizenry.

The Internet has begun to help combating corruption as well. "At this initial stage, online publications would serve as a warning to corrupt political dictators, that news distribution especially via the Internet, is beyond the reach of their iron claws."[26] John Daly notes that the capability could backfire and worries that politicians could use technology to invade privacy and manipulate the message available on the Internet as they have with other technologies.[27] A citizenry unaccustomed to judging the reliability of information could be easily misled. He notes the powerful political websites in the United States and writes, "Politicians, at least, seem convinced that the Internet can help them. But helping politicians may not be enough to help democracy."[28] However, what Daly forgets is that those with "watchdog" mentalities have just as quickly jumped into the cyber age. The Institute for a Democratic Alternative in South Africa (IDASA) launched a website in early February that details the events and documents of the arms deal controversy in South Africa. The site provides information on a controversial and expensive arms deal threatening the South African government's credibility. "The site is intended for journalists, civil society and other citizens who can use it to navigate their way through the current maze of information."[29] Access to the facts is the first step in demanding change.

The U.S. initiatives and ECOWAS could play a role in enhancing this capability. First, the Leland Initiative is working to build connectivity and train Africans in the use of the Internet, and U.S.

policy initiatives work to promote democracy and security. There is no reason for these goals to be mutually exclusive. A company called Unique Solutions organized an Internet-awareness seminar in Banjul, Gambia in February. The event focused on journalism and the Internet. Issues such as privacy, ethics, crime, security, health, and the computer system itself were covered.[30] The Leland Initiative could promote programs like this with the Internet service providers it contracts and make awareness seminars an established part of the contract. ECOWAS leaders and personnel could be contacted by their U.S. counterparts and urged to attend similar sessions on how the media can enhance democracy and how it will make corruption more difficult. Leaders, journalists, and citizens alike will become informed users instead of just connected users. The result would be an injection of information and power into the forces promoting democracy and civil society in Africa.

A Professional Security System

Technology helps entities other than the press to strengthen state and democracy. Law enforcement agencies in West African countries are responsible for maintaining a secure internal atmosphere, and professional law enforcement entities are as important as the professional military standards the United States tries to promote through USEUCOM involvement. Strengthening domestic law enforcement and promoting discussion about what law enforcement in a democracy requires would improve the African community. Modern U.S. law enforcement relies heavily on technology, and an Internet connection would allow cross-jurisdictional dialogue. Such a capability could be established within the West African law enforcement agencies; it would also allow dialogue between West African countries and international law enforcement agencies. For example, mentorship and communication programs could be set up between the Federal Bureau of Investigation and INTERPOL. U.S. law enforcement is bound to benefit from professional contacts in the part of the world heavily involved in both drug and arms trafficking.

In Nigeria, police officers have already learned about the ways technology can supplement their community role. The Police Staff College has developed technology classes to increase crime-fighting ability. The classes include computer appreciation, computer operation and practice, computer applications, Internet connection and web surfing, communication management, IT application in management transformation, and many others. The training is provided by Bitcom

System Limited, a Lagos-based IT solution provider that will provide the support in training and technical requirements that will be needed to keep the center functioning into the future.[31] The Leland Initiative could work with ISPs to expand from this base and have training available for law enforcement in all the communities it wires. Since African police are often involved in national security, a training role for USEUCOM may even be appropriate. Law enforcement in Africa may be known for both its general ineffectiveness and corruption, but providing the best tools to officers will then attract better candidates to the job. Better tools and professional officers have the ability to stabilize a trend of high crime and civil unrest.

Improving Education

One Leland Initiative objective is allowing African ideas to be transmitted to the world. Connecting African journalists, military personnel, law enforcement, and citizens may be a good start, but a concentrated effort to connect universities is also beneficial. The University of Nijmegen, the Netherlands, is attempting to aid African universities in connecting to the Internet. The "idea was borne out of a number of factors. One of them was that most African universities could not access the current scientific literature as published in the international academic journals. Conversely, the African universities could not publish and present their own academic literature beyond the country of origin or the region."[32] The Leland Initiative could work with universities when wiring and eventually utilize university staff to do some of the necessary training. African students and professors would have access to more information and perhaps become more effective citizens and researchers.

The U.S. government's International Military Education and Training Program, IMET, provides security assistance to military students in over 125 allied and friendly nations. The training is designed to improve military-to-military relations, enhance joint operations with U.S. forces, and augment the ability of the trained personnel to maintain democratic values and human rights.[33] The participants must speak English and are exposed to life in the United States and the function of a civilian-controlled military. The training could be expanded to provide military students with exposure to Internet resources on related subjects and general information on computer operations. Similar to the benefits of connecting law enforcement and universities, African military personnel could be in contact with cross-Atlantic colleagues and conduct their own research.

Stronger Economy

Perhaps the most important benefit to be realized from a coordinated effort to wire West Africa, though, would be a revitalized regional economy. Africa is the land that industrialization and development forgot; the prohibitive cost of modern industrialization and problems of disease, hunger, and ethnic tension left the countries struggling to survive. The Internet could play some role in helping to change that historical legacy. The world is shifting away from an economy focused on mere industry toward a system requiring connectivity, and countries that do not start on the road of connectivity will be left behind. A proactive approach to connectivity in African is essential.

Some West African countries have already sensed the trend. Côte d'Ivoire, a traditional economic superstar by West African standards, has two companies providing access to the web, and several newspapers proudly advertise their editions on the web. The business capital, Abidjan, boasts a handful of Internet cafes. "The Internet revolution is propelling countries such as Ivory Coast into effective globalization," one account of these new ventures explains. It has "an extreme importance in the transformation of socio-economic structures."[34] Although there are many problems with the system, such as the cost of both hardware and access, Ivorians are convinced this development will be as prosperous as their revenue-producing cocoa and coffee plants. "I am sure that if access is easier it can help fight poverty. With the Internet, I can set up a business very easily . . ." said Moussa Bakayoko, director of the Ivorian branch of the international nonprofit Internet Society.[35] While such sentiments no doubt reflect only a partial understanding of the challenges involved in Internet-enabled commerce, it nonetheless remains true that African businesses can become more effective with greater connectivity in a global world.

Ghana is using this new market, one that does not require large amounts of industrialization, to become involved in the global economy. Ghanaians are currently processing data in their information sector for American Express and Aetna Healthcare.[36] Again, the Leland Initiative can work with providers to insure incentives and training are available for existing businesses and new companies. George Apenteng, director of Ghana's Institute for Economic Affairs, has pointed out that, "People here want into the global marketplace; they know it's the way out of poverty."[37] The Leland Initiative is in the position to coordinate an initial step into that global marketplace by allowing African business to get connected. ECOWAS's structure and relationships with West African business could facilitate the effort.

Challenges

Africa has incredibly difficult issues to overcome: poverty, disease, and civil conflict. Providing an Internet connection through the Leland Initiative and in conjunction with economic-minded ECOWAS and security-focused USEUCOM can only make a small difference in solving these problems, especially at first. However, any tools that could impel progress toward a more stable and healthy continent are to be welcomed. Pursuing connectivity has its own challenges, from cost to the lack of technical expertise, but they can be addressed with the right experts and programs behind them.

Cost

On a continent as poor as Africa, technology is expensive and it is a luxury. Fifteen million dollars is an excellent start, but it certainly will not buy computers for all of West Africa. Cybercafes are an option, but connection time can be extraordinarily expensive by African standards. "Technology is keeping pace with time, yet universally a lot of people are losing out because information technologies have not factored in accessibility by ordinary people."[38] Fortunately, the Leland Initiative can help with the problem of cost, because direct connection to domestic providers significantly reduces the price of connectivity. In Côte d'Ivoire, a direct domestic link to an ISP provided by the initiative negated the need to first transmit information to the United States via satellite and reduced costs.[39]

ISP's are excited about the development, and one of the company's directors declared that eventually access should be free to users and all costs met by advertisements.[40] Hardware costs are also falling due to an agreement between Côte d'Ivoire and China that will produce less expensive equipment for the Ivorian market. The lesson is that the Leland Initiative can both connect Africa and develop businesses interested in administering the connections and training users: affordability follows when the free market and home governments venture in to make the connection and hardware reasonably priced. Cote d'Ivoire demonstrates these possibilities.

Technical Expertise

Another obstacle in African countries is the availability of technical expertise—although that barrier, too, has a solution. As universities become wired through proposed Leland projects, students will become educated in computer technology and be available for both the work force and as community liaisons bridging the digital divide. Tunisia began a communications and information technology-training program for new Master's graduates to expose them to the technologies and make them more employable.[41] The effort is underway across other parts of Africa as well. Eighteen Internet administrators participated in an Internet training program in Benin sponsored by the United Nations.[42] The finance and economy minister of Benin, Abdoulaye Bio Tchane, remarked, "How can we make progress if we do not have national expertise, with well-trained and competent people capable of ensuring reliable and sustainable maintenance of computer hardware, information systems and networks?"

Cisco, a leading hardware supplier, agrees and has sponsored programs exposing Africans to the computer. The company is working to expand its training academies to 48 states around the world, and the Information Technology Center at the University of Ouagadougou in Burkina Faso will become another Regional Academy for the Cisco initiative.[43] Again, it shows that if the United States can make a concerted effort to facilitate connections, the free market and the human drive for improvement will overcome other obstacles.

Conclusion

The United States has lofty goals in Africa. Although recognizing virtually no traditional security interests, it is still dedicating security personnel, funding, and equipment to the countries. Through that effort, the United States hopes to achieve the USEUCOM articulated goals of free, stable, and prosperous nations through a strategic concept of "Shape, Respond, and Prepare." The Leland Initiative seeks to create sustainable Internet programs that will increase the African capacity to use information. U.S. policy overall seeks to promote peace, provide humanitarian assistance, foster democracy and human rights, and support growth and sustainable development.

Increasing Internet connections in ECOWAS states can help to achieve these goals by taking advantage of ECOWAS relationships and efforts. A more concerted effort by the Leland Initiative to put the tools in the hands of professionals and citizens alike will foster democracy, increase security, and enhance the economy. Democracy will follow the increased information flow the Internet can provide. Professional, downsized militaries and professional, effective law enforcement will enhance the security atmosphere in West African countries. And, finally, economic advantages to connection provide a possible way for Africa to enter the global marketplace as a viable, productive member. Challenges of expense and technical expertise will be overcome as the free market performs, and businesses and universities sponsor programs to make the technology a more valuable investment.

Critics may note that Africa does not need the Internet; it needs vaccinations, food, and safe water. Others will say that Africa does not need the connection to grow; it requires an end to ethnic strife, corruption, and politicized militaries. However, Africa may realize a glimpse of democratic practices, a more stable security system, and economic promise through the Internet. The United States will benefit when military resources can be used elsewhere and business opportunities surface. More importantly, though, the United States will be pursuing the approach it has long professed but unevenly followed: It will be helping Africans help themselves.

Notes

1. President Clinton, "Building a US-Africa Partnership: Hand-in-Hand for the 21st Century," speech before the National Summit on Africa, U.S. Department of State: Office of Public Diplomacy—Africa and Office of International Information Programs, February 17, 2000, 2.
2. President Clinton, excerpts from remarks at signing of Joint Declaration, Presidential Village, Abuja, Nigeria, "Building a U.S.–Africa Partnership: Hand-in-Hand for the 21st Century," August 26, 2000, 3.
3. Office of International Security Affairs-Department of Defense, "U.S. Security Strategy for Sub-Saharan Africa," *Defense Issues* 10, no. 78 (August 1995), accessed April 13, 2001, http://www.defenselink.mil/speeches/1995/s19950801-report.html.
4. Ibid.
5. USAID Leland Initiative homepage, accessed April 19, 2000, http://www.usaid.gov/regions/afr/leland.
6. Office of International Security Affairs-Department of Defense, "U.S. Security Strategy for Sub-Saharan Africa Africa."
7. USAID Leland Initiative homepage, "Project Description and FAQ," accessed April 19, 2001, http://www.usaid.gov/regions/afr/leland/project.htm.
8. Ibid.
9. United States European Command, "Strategy of Preparedness and Engagement in Africa," accessed April 19, 2001, http://www.eucom.mil/africa/publications/STRATEGY.HTM.
10. Susan E. Rice, Assistant Secretary, Office of Secretary of State: Resources, Plans and Policy, U.S. Department of State, "Request by Region, Sub-Saharan Africa. Bureau of African Affairs," *Congressional Budget Justification for Foreign Operations, Fiscal Year 2001*, released March 15, 2000, www.state.gov/www/budget/fy2001/fn150/forops_full/150fy01_fo_africa.html.

11. CIA 2000 Factbook, accessed May 9, 2001, http://www.odci.gov/cia/publications/factbook/geos/sg.html.
12. Official website of ECOWAS, accessed April 13, 2001, www.ecowas.int/index2.htm.
13. Ibid.
14. Official website of ECOWAS, "Achievements of ECOWAS," accessed April 13, 2001, www.ecowas.int/sitecedeao/english/peace.htm.
15. Ibid.
16. Ibid.
17. Rice, "Congressional Budget Justification."
18. Ibid.
19. Jim Fisher-Thompson, "U.N. Important to U.S.-Africa Peacekeeping Goals, U.S. Official Says," January 11, 2000, http://www.eucom/mil/africa/usis/00jan12htm.
20. Thomas L. Friedman, "Low-Tech Democracy," *New York Times,* accessed May 1, 2001, http://www.nytimes.com.
21. Nana Akufo-Addo quoted by Friedman, "Low-Tech Democracy."
22. Friedman, "Low-Tech Democracy."
23. Ibid.
24. JournalismNet, "The Web and Democracy in Africa," May 5, 2001, http://www.journalismnet.com/tips/africa2000.htm.
25. Ibid.
26. Claudia Anthony, "The Role of Online Publication in the Promotion of Democracy," *ExpoTimes-Freetown,* accessed March 30, 2000, http://allafrica.com/stories/printable/200103300095.html.
27. John A. Daly, "Will the Internet Promote Democracy?" September 2000, http://www.cisp.org/imp/september_2000/daly/09_00daly.htm.
28. Ibid.
29. "IDASA Launches Website to Monitor Controversial Arms Deal," *Panafrican News Agency* (Dakar), February 12, 2001, http://allafrica.com/stories/printable/200102130058.html.
30. "Unique Solutions Organizes Internet Awareness Course for Journalists," *Daily Observer Banjul,* February, 13, 2001, http://allafrica.com/storiees/printable/200102130122.html.
31. Oluwatosin Johnson, "Police Seek IT Skills for National Security," *This Day Lagos,* March 22, 2001, http://allafrica.com/stories/printable/200103220263.html.
32. "Universities to Benefit From New Education Concept," *Panafrican News Agency* (Dakar), February 17, 2001, http://allafrica.com/stories/printable/200102170013.html.
33. Rice, "Congressional Budget Justification."
34. Anthony Morland, "Cote d'Ivoire Accelerates Along Information Highway," *Agence France Presse,* May 21, 1998, document FTS19980521000696, Foreign Broadcast Information Service (FBIS).
35. Ibid.
36. Thomas L. Friedman, "Protesting for Whom?" *New York Times,* 24 April 2001.
37. Ibid.
38. Technology for People—An International Competition," *Accra Mail,* February 5, 2001, http://allafrica.com/stories/printable/200102050299.html.
39. Morland, "Cote d'Ivoire Accelerates Along Information Highway."
40. Ibid.
41. "Bid Steps Up for Information Technology," *Panafrican News Agency* (Tunisia), April 13, 2001, http://allafrica.com/stories/printable/200104130100.html.

42. "Internet Trainers' Course in Cotonou," *Panafrican News Agency* (Dakar), January 29, 2001, http://allafrica.com/stories/printable200101290102.
43. Ibid.

About the Authors

Emil T. Bailey, Jr., is a program manager/senior analyst at Corporate Risk International, an international security consulting firm, where he manages an online open-source intelligence service for multinational corporations. He is a masters candidate in the Security Studies Program at Georgetown University. He earned his bachelor's degree in political science from West Virginia University, where he graduated magna cum laude.

Alessandra Cabras is a research analyst at the Washington, D.C.-based Global Coalition for Africa (GCA). Previously she worked for the United Nations, serving in Cambodia in 1993, in South Africa in 1994, and in Burundi from 1994 through 1996. She is currently an MA candidate in the Security Studies Program at Georgetown University. The views expressed are her own and do not reflect the policy or position of GCA.

Glenn Hickok served as a U.S. Navy pilot for ten years. He completed tours in the Pentagon developing requirements for future naval aviation capabilities and assessing the strategic implications of funding deficiencies in readiness programs. He is a distinguished graduate of the Security Studies Program at Georgetown University, where he focused on global strategy. He currently is employed by EMC and serves on the business advisory committee for the Lexington Institute, a nonprofit, nonpartisan, public-policy research organization headquartered in Arlington, Virginia.

Richard Hughes, a 1992 graduate of the United States Naval Academy, served upon commissioning as a helicopter pilot and staff officer for the

Chief of Naval Operations. Mr. Hughes currently works for Austin International Consulting in Arlington, Virginia. He is a distinguished graduate of the Security Studies Program at Georgetown University.

Sudhir Mahara was commissioned at the Royal Military Academy, Sandhurst, UK, in 1990 and served in the Royal Nepalese Army until 1999. He was trained in special operations at the U.S. Army JFK Special Warfare School and Center and served on the policy staff of the Chief of the Nepalese Army for internal security analysis and planning. He served as an operations officer for the United Nations Interim Force in Lebanon (UNIFIL) in 1996 and was an instructor for peace support operations training in 1999. He has a masters in security studies from Georgetown University and a second masters in political science from Tribhuvan University, Kathmandu.

Michael J. Mazarr is a professor of national security strategy at the U.S. National War College. He is also an adjunct professor in the Security Studies Program at Georgetown University and co-founder of The Archigos Project, a nonprofit organization dealing with leadership issues. He has been a senior fellow at the Center for Strategic and International Studies and president of the Henry L. Stimson Center. He is the author of ten books and numerous essays on international security affairs. The views expressed in his chapter are his own and do not reflect the opinions of the War College or the U.S. government.

Glenn McCormick is a 1977 graduate in physics from the U.S. Naval Academy and holds a masters degree in system management from the University of Southern California. He served as an F-14 pilot in the U.S. Navy and currently flies 767 aircraft for American Airlines.

Ryan McMichael earned his bachelor of science degree from the Institute of Optics at the University of Rochester in 1994 and his masters from the Edmund A. Walsh School of Foreign Service, Georgetown University, in 2001. He is employed as an engineer with Photon Research Associates, Inc., of San Diego, supporting the Department of Defense.

Amanda Olson works for a Washington, DC-based defense consulting firm. She has written country reports on African states for the U.S. Army and currently supports future concept development for the U.S. Air Force. A graduate of the University of Wisconsin with a B.S. in history and political science, she is currently earning a masters degree in national security at Georgetown University. She is a member of Women in International Security (WIIS).

Tania Stanley O'Neil is an international security analyst with the Department of Defense, where she has worked since 1995. Before coming to the Department of Defense she worked for two years at the Department of Commerce and has also worked in the U.S. House of Representatives. She holds an M.A. in national security studies from Georgetown University and a B.A. in international studies from York College of Pennsylvania. The views expressed in her article are those of the author and do not reflect the position or policy of the Department of Defense or the U.S. government.

Robert Peters graduated cum laude from Miami University with a bachelor's degree in political science and history and went on to receive his M.A. with distinction in national security studies from Georgetown University. He is currently employed as a research associate by an Arlington, Virginia–based think tank.

Michael Rabasco was most recently a senior foreign affairs and military advisor to a member of Congress. He earned a masters degree with a focus on Middle East security from Georgetown University's Security Studies Program in 2001 and received his undergraduate degree from Saint Michael's College in 1992. Michael is a member of the Middle East Institute and speaks Farsi.

Index